Happy birthday
1979.

Eight Flat-Racing Stables

JOHN RICKMAN

Eight Flat-Racing Stables

HEINEMANN : LONDON

ALSO BY JOHN RICKMAN

Homes of Sport: Horse Racing

William Heinemann Limited
15 Queen Street, Mayfair, London W1X 8BE

LONDON   MELBOURNE   TORONTO
JOHANNESBURG   AUCKLAND

First published 1979
© John Rickman 1979
SBN 434 63710 6

Printed and bound in Great Britain by
Morrison & Gibb Ltd, London and Edinburgh

Contents

List of Illustrations

Introduction

The Light Houses,
Lowlandman's Bay,
Isle of Jura, Argyll.

With the extended coverage made possible by TV, we know much
more about the looks, voices and views of key people in the world
of racing than we did in the past. Even so, our curiosity is often
merely titillated and we want to know much, much more about
them, whether they be professionals, amateurs, owners or trainers
—not forgetting the horses, too. Though it must be admitted that
if anything comes from the mouths of the last-named it is not
always reliable and it is certainly second-hand!

Because of the pace of live TV racing coverage, interviewers are
rarely given time to extract more than a few sentences from
interviewees. I did the job for more than twenty-six years and I
know how restricting are the flight of time and certain conventions.
It is not often that a leading racing personality, a champion or
maestro, is featured in a carefully prepared TV piece of as much as
half an hour, as was the case in Julian Wilson's talk with Sir Noel
Murless, a great trainer on the brink of his retirement. I dare say
this TV interview was appreciated and enjoyed by thousands, but
such work is uncommon.

So we are back where we started. The viewer's interest and
thirst for knowledge is aroused but not always satisfied by an
entertaining live racecourse interview on TV. I suppose it can also
be said, with some cynicism, that far from being interesting, some
interviewees are boring and others have not the ability to make
the best of themselves on the box.

This brings me to why I wrote this book. Heinemann suggested
that I should tell people as much as I could about some of the

leading flat-race trainers so that when they are seen on TV viewers may know much more of their backgrounds and therefore savour what is said and seen in the interviews. I have attempted to fulfil this brief.

'Know your enemy' is a tag which fighting men recognise as extremely important. Not for a moment do I suggest that trainers are the enemies of punters, but the greater a punter's knowledge of a trainer's character, training methods, his preferences for certain types of horses, the jockeys he employs, his favourite courses, those at which he is most successful and those where he has achieved legs of doubles and sometimes trebles, the greater chance that punter has of backing winners and, at the same time, acquiring valuable and entertaining Turf intelligence.

With this in mind, I asked Dorothy Laird, a racing writer and author of several books about the Turf, if she would compile some statistics about each of the trainers in this book. She has extracted some most fascinating facts from the records, as readers will see. The figures are up to date—to the end of the 1978 season.

I also owe debts of gratitude to the eight trainers featured in this book. Their help has been unstinted. I am happy too to have visited their homes and to have met members of their families and staff. I also take off my hat to trainers' wives. My visits have served to remind me how helpful they are to their husbands in their demanding profession. The Yorkshire trainer Michael Easterby was outspoken about how 'a good wife' can make a man, and I have quoted his words in the text.

I selected the trainers who are featured in this book chiefly as a result of my publisher's suggestions. The remaining two or three played themselves into the side, so to speak.

I hope I may also be allowed to take this opportunity to thank several hundred trainers for the help and trust extended to me during many years in my work with the *Gloucestershire Echo*, the *Daily Sketch*, the *Daily Mail*, BBC and ITV. I have had many friends among the ranks of trainers and still have. I wish I could write about them all. Well, I will not give up just yet!

Lastly I offer my warmest thanks to three women who have helped me tremendously: they are Peggy, my wife, Hilary Gould who did the typing, and Alicia Yerburgh who did the editing.

xii

Henry Cecil

of Warren Place, Newmarket

One of the most interesting Newmarket training stables for a horse-loving racing journalist to visit is Warren Place, with its luxurious trainer's house and well-built, airy boxes.

This establishment stands aloof on the hill to the east of the town. I have had the pleasure of being entertained there for more than thirty years; first by Sam Armstrong, whose horses were always superbly trained and whose gin-and-french had a kick almost as strong as the 'bombs' of the one-time Malton trainer Rufus Beasley. The blast of a couple of these rendered the return journey to York quite painless, as I well remember in pre-breathalyser days.

After Sam Armstrong came Sir Noel Murless, whose hospitality and horses were also of a high standard. The comparatively new master of Warren Place is Henry Cecil, stepson of a famous trainer, Sir Cecil Boyd-Rochfort, and son-in-law of Sir Noel Murless, another master of his craft.

Henry has an 'air'. There is something about him that makes him stand out in a crowd. He has charm, style, dresses well and, most important, has in ten years gone to the top of his profession. His background is such that he is perfectly equipped to train for anyone. He lived as a baby at Crathes Castle, Kincardineshire, and is, in fact, half Scottish. He has worked hard as a member of the rank and file in studs in Europe and America. He was also assistant trainer for several years to Sir Cecil Boyd-Rochfort.

As we sat together one December morning, after Second Lot, in his light, spacious and comfortable drawing-room, Henry came

Henry Cecil with his father-in-law, Sir Noel Murless, at Ascot.
(Desmond O'Neill)

quickly to the point and asked me what I wanted to talk about. I replied that I would like to discuss several aspects of his life as a trainer and the ability and character of a few of the better horses he has had through his hands.

Henry, so to speak, fairly pinged out of stalls with, 'Within certain bounds I really don't mind what people say about me and what you write about me! Go ahead, ask me what you like, eh?

But before you do, let me give you one or two more of my beliefs . . . To be in the top flight as a trainer you have to be ambitious. I am ambitious. I don't want to be an also ran. One must have a ruthless streak and the competitive spirit. On the other hand I like to see my friends doing well, eh?'

I will not embellish those remarks for though they tell us perhaps not all we want to know about Henry, they outline much of his character. He went on, 'You don't want to write a lot of dull facts about me and my horses. You want to make it light and amusing.' I made no reply for I believed that my job was to report his views. Henry being the taut, mercurial young man that he is, what he cares to say is unlikely to be dull.

After Henry's opening dash we settled down to a more conventional pace. I have always believed that whatever a man's profession, how he started on his way to the top and how he got there, is usually interesting, sometimes fascinating. In Henry's case there was no running away from home to seek fame and fortune but there was a similarity between the path he took early in his career and that followed by Jeremy Hindley. Both young men went into the stud side of racing. Both found that for them it lacked excitement and were attracted more by the colour and the thrills of training and the racecourse.

Henry told me, 'I enjoyed horses from an early age. I had several ponies and I liked the flashy ones best. After I left Canford where I was at school, the idea seemed to be that I should become a stud manager but because of my age—people seemed to prefer retired colonels to run their studs—I didn't get very far. I did two seasons at Lord Derby's stud, Woodlands, and two at Marcus Wickham-Boynton's Burton Agnes stud. I worked in France for Madame Couturié and at Mr Jock Whitney's Greentree stud, in America. I also did two spells at the Equine Research Station here at Newmarket. At the end of all this there did not seem anything for me to do but luckily my step-father Cecil Boyd-Rochfort wanted someone to help him. He was getting on in years. I was his assistant trainer for about five years at Freemason Lodge, in the Bury road here at Newmarket.

'My father was killed in the War. My mother Rohays brought us to live near Newmarket when I was about two and, as you know,

3

married Cecil Boyd-Rochfort. I didn't think that being one of five children I would ever be in the financial position to find enough capital to start training. I didn't think I'd get the chance so that's why I went on the stud side. I've never regretted not persevering with it. Joining my step-father at Freemason Lodge was the turning point because when he retired I took over.'

I asked Henry if he found Sir Cecil a strict and hard boss, remembering as I did that Bruce Hobbs assisted The Captain as he was usually called, for several years before Henry's time. Henry told me, 'I got him in his slightly more mellow days. He was easier to work with when I went to him than earlier on. He was always a strict disciplinarian but very fair. He gave me more responsibility than some of my predecessors. I married Julie in 1966 when I was still assistant trainer at £5 a week.

'I learned the basic ideas about training from Cecil but being with a great expert like him I tended also to develop my own ideas. For instance his stable management was something out of the past. The way things were done at Freemason Lodge is obviously not done now. I couldn't hope to carry on in the same way with the staff. These days one has to be more intimate with staff. Obviously there is a dividing line between master and man but now one has to be more familiar with one's workers. One must understand them and be among them more than was the case in the old days. It's rather like being a troop or platoon commander in the Army. You have to be with your men and at the same time command them and earn their respect. You simply cannot treat men just like numbers as was so often done in the past—not only in racing stables, I might add.'

When the time came to begin training in 1969, many of The Captain's owners left an animal or two with Henry. Luckily for him one of those horses was Wolver Hollow, owned by Cecil Boyd-Rochfort and bequeathed to him by the late Mrs Hope Iselin, a wealthy American. She lived to be 101. She had been a patron for many years and Cecil Boyd-Rochfort was very fond of her. Another horse Henry had was Approval, with which he won the Observer Gold Cup worth £19,624. As Wolver Hollow won the Eclipse (£25,829) Henry got off to a flying start.

Cecil Boyd-Rochfort had trained Wolver Hollow, named after Mrs Iselin's Long Island home, as a two-, three- and four-year-old. He had problems with this son of Sovereign Path. The Captain always said he was a good horse in the making but he had digestive troubles and lacked a bit of confidence. He improved with age. The colt did not win as a juvenile although he was runner-up to the smart Falcon, at Royal Ascot. Mrs Iselin suggested to The Captain that she might race the colt in America. The suggestion was not followed up when Wolver Hollow promptly won at Folkestone and York and was third in the Cambridgeshire (1967) with 8 st 1 lb. In 1968 he won at Deauville and with 9 st 8 lb was beaten a neck by Emerilo (20 to 1), in the Cambridgeshire. The winner, trained by Percy Allden, received 27 lb from Wolver Hollow.

Henry took up the fascinating Wolver Hollow story with, 'He had a lot of ability and speed but because of his problems he was unpredictable. As a five-year-old I thought he would win the Lockinge Stakes at Newbury which was, in fact, won by Habitat. Why I gave Wolver Hollow such a good chance was because he had worked so well with that fine sprinter Tower Walk, trained by Geoff Barling. I said to Stan Smith who was riding work for me, "Look, this work will be too short for my horse. Sit behind. If you are going well, keep in touch and don't call on him too much because we are only working for about five furlongs". But he went past Tower Walk, a six-to-seven-furlong horse, as if he was standing still.'

Understandably Henry thought that wherever Tower Walk finished in the Lockinge, Wolver Hollow would be a long way in front of him. When it came to the race Tower Walk was just beaten by Habitat and Jimmy Reppin. 'My horse was more or less tailed off. That was all wrong,' Henry told me, 'but then he won the Eclipse which showed what a really good horse he was. Many people said that Park Top was unlucky not to win. I know that Piggott rode Wolver Hollow beautifully, coming up on the inside, but in my view it was his day and he would have won anyhow. He cantered up but, you know, he was like his son Wollow—once he had beaten the opposition that was it. It did not do to bring him to the front too soon to win his race.'

Wolver Hollow (Lester Piggott) wins the Eclipse Stakes from Park Top (G. Lewis). (Sport & General)

A number of racing writers did not rate Wolver Hollow very highly. This is because many of them did not realise he had been so delicate and that he could be a good horse, as seen in the Eclipse. As Henry said, 'Wolver Hollow was a good one all right but not in the same class as Wollow, but, of course, he has done very well at stud. When you think Wolver Hollow nearly died at the end of his three-year-old career—he wasted away to nothing— he did pretty well to recover and win as a four-year-old and then in 1969 to win the Eclipse—and very nearly to win the Cambridgeshire with 9 st 8 lb in 1968.

'Many of Princely Gift's descendants do best if held up for a last furlong run and Wolver Hollow was no exception,' said Henry. 'Once in front they become lazy and you have to keep them going with the result that frequently when winning they look unimpressive but, believe me, horses such as Wolver Hollow and Wollow were very impressive if you watched them carefully. They revealed this brilliance when, shall we say, running fourth or fifth, they were pulled out and made up the ground terribly quickly. One moment the horse was fifth and a few seconds later he was two lengths in front. He seemed to come from behind and take the lead in a twinkling of an eye. This is the sign of a good horse.'

Henry then switched back to May 1969 when he had his first winner, Celestial Cloud, ridden by Bill O'Gorman in the Newby Amateur Riders' Stakes at Ripon. 'Actually,' he said, 'I think my first winner was a loser. There was no photograph finish. I think he was second really but the judge gave it to him.

'At that time we were beginning to wonder if we would ever have a winner. It seemed months and months before we did.' ('Actually it was the seventeenth of May,' said Julie.)

Henry confessed, 'I used to listen to other people on the stands when we had a runner. Someone was bound to say "No, don't back that thing of Henry Cecil's. He can't train ivy up the wall." When Celestial Cloud won I very nearly cried it was such a relief.' Many of us have experienced exactly that emotion and have not been able to hide a tear or two. Well, what's the harm in that?

'I remember before I had a winner my father-in-law, Sir Noel

Murless, was very kind to me,' Henry told me. 'He felt rather sorry for me on the Heath once and said to me as my horses came up past us, "Look here, Henry, those horses come up the gallop like a lot of old gentlemen. To win races nowadays they've got to really work at home. They have got to be absolutely fit."

'So after that I decided to do a little more with my horses and the results started coming along. I know that Noel was very worried about telling me because he did not want to interfere but I realised I would have to change my methods. Noel has been a great help to me in the past and he still is. If I am worried about something I have to talk to him.'

Henry then told me that he didn't care much for early two-year-olds and that normally he had very few of them. He is not particularly interested in sprinters although when one comes his way it is well trained and raced.

'I have never had a top sprinter except New Model. He was a good one but he was more of a seven-furlong horse really. Most of the horses I get are potential staying three-year-olds. These I love. We have had a lot of luck with the few really good stayers we have had.

'We have won plenty of Cup races. I don't like horses that make two-year-olds and then you wave them goodbye. I appreciate horses that stay with you and develop. You get to know them and their careers are based over two, three, four or even five years, rather than one year.' Henry has trained several horses including Fool's Mate and Arisaig which have won in four consecutive seasons.

'I'm not interested in betting'—he is also teetotal—'and my only hope of making money is to have potentially good horses which go to stud. Then I hope that I get a share in them. If one has an interest in four or five horses standing at stud at once, well, there's a good source of income. I can tell you that is needed because as you can imagine Warren Place is very expensive to keep up with its gardens and grounds.'

I asked Henry who among owners were a great help to him early in his career. His answer was, 'I have very few of the original patrons left. There is Mrs Hope Hanes. She is still with me. Also

8

Mrs Stanhope Joel and Julie's mother Gwen Murless. Most of my present-day owners are comparatively new but I have been extremely lucky with them. If you look through my list you will see I have the type of owner who really understands racing and who has been in the game a long time. This is a tremendous help because I don't think I'm very good with people. I've got owners like the Macdonald Buchanans, Lord Howard de Walden, Mr Jim Joel, Mrs Stanhope Joel, Marcus Wickham-Boynton, the Hornungs, Mrs Peter Burrell and a few others. It is great fun training for them. You can discuss problems with them and they know what you are talking about.

'There are not many of the new type of owner coming into racing who really understand the game. But of course it is a trainer's job to help them learn more about racing. After all they employ us to train their horses and it is up to us to see they get a fair deal and enjoy being an owner. Most of the high-priced yearlings we buy are for foreigners. We spend comparatively little money for the majority of our English owners.'

When Henry goes to a sale to buy a few yearlings he has already done several hours' homework on the catalogue. 'Quite honestly,' he told me, 'I like buying my own yearlings. I made a lot of mistakes early on but by now I think I have a pretty good idea of what's required. Charles St George has been a great help to me. He has had horses for years and has introduced me to a lot of decent owners including Mr Bunker Hunt. I hope they will continue to buy yearlings for us to train.

'About sixty per cent of my annual intake of yearlings are home-bred which is immensely important, but it is always thrilling to be able to buy ten or twelve colts. Here again I must thank Noel because some of the nice horses I have bought are through him. Then there is Mr Carlo D'Alessio. He is another one who doesn't breed so one buys for him—such horses as Aliante and Wollow, winner of the 1976 Two Thousand Guineas.'

Incidentally Henry did not buy his 1975 Two Thousand Guineas winner, Bolkonski. He was sent to him as an early three-year-old after running in Italy, where he won over a mile on heavy ground in November 1974.

Bolkonski (G. Dettori) being led in after winning the 2,000 Guineas at Newmarket. (Sport & General)

'Some years in the past,' Henry went on, 'I've gone to the sales without any orders at all and bought on spec. I've usually managed to dispose of them. This year I suppose I have spent more than £500,000 at the sales.'

'When you have got those horses in your yard what do you give them to eat?' I asked, knowing that not all trainers have the same ideas about feeding. Henry's answer was, however, a fairly standard one although he did make some interesting points. 'We are basic feeders. I am very fussy about good hay. We buy the best we can get—hay and oats. We do not feed a lot of supplements. But we do give them some—for instance Chevronel which has trace elements in it. This is useful in a bad year for hay—when the hay is just lacking something. If they do not require the supplements then the body rejects them and there is no harm done.'

Henry's head man is Paddy Rudkin who was for some years in the same job with Joe Lawson, trainer of Never Say Die. His travelling head man is Arthur Simmonds who learned his trade with Frank Butters, one of the greats of my time. Jim White, travelling head lad for Sir Noel Murless for many years, lives at Warren Place and still lends a hand. Henry's secretary is Ann Scriven. 'She runs the whole show really,' said Henry with one of his charming smiles as Ann joined us in front of the fire. 'I'm just the wooden thing on the front of a ship. What do you call it? The figurehead? Yes, that's it. No, Ann runs the business.'

Ann learned her job with The Captain. She told me, 'I've been here since 1953. I always wanted a job with horses and what better place to be than with a top stable at Newmarket!' She comes from Guildford and was very interested in racing before she arrived at Headquarters, as Newmarket is known in the racing world. 'The breeding side of racing has always fascinated me. Sorry to say I have not got a mare of my own but I've got a hack which I ride out with the string every morning. I didn't ride for about twenty-one years because The Captain wasn't keen on my riding out just for pleasure. That was a bit frowned on!' she said.

Ann's job, as Henry acknowledges, is an important one because he spends little more than ten minutes in the office each day, which leaves plenty of back-up work for Ann, and Julie.

I next asked Henry what he thought about the pattern of racing generally. Could it be improved? 'It most certainly can,' he replied, 'I think there is too much of taking the merit away from a horse. The very good horses are few and far between. The Group races are fine for them, but the good horse, the one that misses say by 10 lb being among the best, is top of every handicap, and the chances are that he is not a great weight carrier. I think they have taken the merit away from those horses completely.'

He hammered home his point. 'There should be more condition races for those good horses which have not won a Group 1 or Group 2 race because in handicaps they have to carry ten stone and give away the best part of three stone to some horses which in my view are not a good advertisement for British racing. It is usually asking the very useful to good horse to do too much.

'I am all for Pattern Races. I think they are a very good idea. The whole basis of selling horses well, and the stallion structure, lies in these prestige races.

'I run a lot of horses in handicaps. They are nearly always high in the weights because they run on their merits and are thoroughly exposed. I know we have won plenty of handicaps but I think that there should be more condition races for the horses which just get beaten in Group races. They are crucified in handicaps.'

One of the answers to Henry's problem—probably the only one —is the Limited Handicap, advocated by the Newmarket Trainers' Federation and implemented by the Jockey Club. Jeremy Hindley, whose paper on this subject did much to persuade the Jockey Club to introduce this type of race in 1977, also talked with me on this point. I have included what he said in his chapter in this book.

Henry next launched off into the realm of good and very good horses which he had trained in nine years.

'Approval,' he said, 'was a very good horse, but I am afraid he was not quite genuine. Falkland was another very good horse. I always thought he was unlucky not to have won the St Leger. He was ridden by Greville Starkey. The race was won by Athens Wood, superbly ridden by Lester Piggott. He dominated the race and the other jockeys fell for it. I know it was a great race to watch but Piggott set too slow a pace and they all followed him like sheep. When Piggott quickened up with a furlong and a half to go Falkland was run off his feet. Then he came right back and tried unsuccessfully to come between two horses in what was a blanket finish. He was just beaten. I shall always believe he should have won. He was only a neck and a head behind Athens Wood and Homeric.

'Relay Race was one of my better horses. He was a bit of a cripple and used to spend most of his time in a swimming bath in Gloucestershire. He was practically last into the straight in Morston's Derby and then finished just behind the placed horses. He won the Jockey Club Cup and the Hardwicke Stakes. He would have been a very good horse if he had been sound.

'Bolkonski was an outstanding miler. He won the Guineas not just because Grundy, whom he beat, had been laid up. I think he would have beaten him anyway because he—Bolkonski—a brilliant miler, was taking on a very good mile-and-a-half horse—Grundy. Nine times out of ten there could only be one result to that contest.

Bolkonski narrowly wins the 2,000 Guineas from Grundy, who is almost entirely obscured by him. (Sport & General)

'A lot of people said that the form of Bolkonski (by Balidar) made him a better horse than Wollow but I can tell you that Wollow was a much superior horse.

'Let me compare these two Guineas winners. I would say that Bolkonski was a very good horse, a nice horse to look at, but in character he was much more highly strung than Wollow. Bolkonski was always "working", always doing something, walking or trotting. He was never relaxed. He tended to sweat. When he walked he was always on the bit. In no way could he have lasted the whole season at his prime. He came right and was at his best for about two months.

'Wollow was much more placid and relaxed. He never did more than he had to. You could train him over longer periods. Considering he was immature and weak he was obviously brilliant, because to win six Group 1 races was quite something. He would have been a much better four-year-old but he was sold before the Derby and he went to stud at the end of his three-year-old career. I must underline the fact that he raced so marvellously well as a very immature horse.'

Wollow is by Wolver Hollow out of Wichurajana, by Worden II, and in my view he was not bred to be a two-year-old but he was unbeaten at that age. His dam was a half sister of Exar, placed in the Ascot Gold Cup.

'People tended to make Wollow into a world beater,' Henry said. 'As I say, he was unbeaten as a two-year-old and he won the Greenham and the Guineas in his second season. Then he flopped in the Derby and many of the people who praised him to the skies were the first to condemn him, but I'll tell you this, he did something after his Derby failure that many horses do not do. He came right back. He was second in the Eclipse and got the race when Trepan was disqualified. He then won the Sussex Stakes at Goodwood followed by the Benson and Hedges Gold Cup, over one and a quarter miles at York, beating Crow, subsequently the Leger winner. He thoroughly recovered his prestige after people had been so quick to knock him on the head.'

I sensed that Henry was more than pleased that Wollow had done much to silence his critics and I am bound to say that his feelings were understandable and justified.

'To go back to the Derby,' Henry resumed, 'he flopped behind Empery. I think it was Nature just taking its course, making him say, so to speak, "At this stage I've had enough. I cannot do it." Don't forget that he was immature. He had done enough for the time being.

'Another interesting point is that he had never worked so well as he did before the Derby. I thought he would stay the mile and a half because he was so relaxed. Quite honestly I thought it was just a case of his going down and coming back—the winner. We did not make excuses at the time but in the race he bent one of his plates backwards. He had three or four inches of this sticking straight into the ground every time he put his foot down.

'People said he looked light at the Derby. Absolute rubbish. In any case he never was a massive colt. I thought that when he

Jockey Dettori waves to the crowd as Wollow is led in by his owner Mr D'Alessio after winning the 2,000 Guineas. (Sport & General)

went to the race he was in tremendous form. It could be that his bad draw affected him. Dettori had to bustle him to get a position. He was a horse that liked to be off the bit and then picked up to make his run but he was in a hopeless position coming into the straight. I would not want to blame the jockey. The only reason I can give is that he had a lapse which a horse will do if he is immature—and that of all days was the day he had it!

'Wollow was a real gentleman of a horse. He had that air which good horses so often have. When horses go into the parade ring before a race most of them just troop in one behind the other but not Wollow. He would stop, put his head in the air, look round, sum everything up and then quietly walk on. He was definitely a leader of the herd. He had a great presence. He was not just another horse. He was a very intelligent horse which is not a remark I can make about Bolkonski although in some ways he was sensible and behaved himself. Bolkonski was second in the Craven Stakes, won the Guineas, the St James's Palace Stakes and the Sussex Stakes. When he won at Goodwood it was the best race of his life for he beat Lianga and Rose Bowl. That was the end of him. He had got into a terrible state and was useless.

'Wollow was so relaxed we could do exactly what we wanted to do with him. Bolkonski, if he needed a steady canter, well, you could give it to him, but he was doing much more than that underneath, which is why it was so difficult to keep him at his best for more than a few weeks. He burned himself out. Incidentally he had a one-sided mouth. He went off to stand at stud in France.'

It is good to learn that as I write these lines Wollow has had his first foal, a bay filly out of Paravant, by the Derby winner Parthia, and out of Nanavati, by Nearco. The filly was bred by the Italian company Allevamento Pegasus. The foal, like her sire, is a bay. Her grandsire Wolver Hollow was a pure breeding bay. Wollow, who stands at the Banstead Manor Stud, has now had time to mature and could prove a great sire.

Henry, who talked at times passionately about the two Guineas winners which have helped him to found his reputation as a successful trainer, then went on to another of his equine friends, Lucky Wednesday.

16

'Lucky Wednesday would have been an outstanding horse if he had raced on really soft ground,' he said, 'but he never had that in 1977 at all. I think he would have won the Eclipse but he couldn't go on that going which was officially "firm". He broke the Sandown track record on ground which he hated but when he got good ground, as at Royal Ascot, he won like a very good horse. He broke down because we had to train and race him on ground that didn't suit him.'

He must have been an outstanding mile-and-a-quarter horse for he beat Relkino at level weights in Sandown's Westbury Stakes on firm ground in April 1977. Next he beat Norfolk Air in the Clive Graham Stakes at Goodwood in May. Then on ground more to his liking he won the Prince of Wales Stakes at Royal Ascot, very easily. After this came the race which probably put paid to his future as a racehorse—the Eclipse Stakes run on the firm ground which he abominated. This was won by Artaius. He lopped .39 of a second off the course record and Lucky Wednesday was only one and a half lengths behind him.

To be champion trainer with more than a hundred winners ten years after first holding a licence is a fine feat. This Henry Cecil achieved in 1978, without winning a classic.

Henry's views on the 1978 performance of his team are as follows: 'Some years my two-year-olds seem to be able to run. Then the next year they don't. This season they have been good. On the other hand the three-year-olds generally have not been so good. Apart from Gunner B who won five races and £84,307 in stakes, and two or three other senior horses, my strength, as I say, has been two-year-olds but I find it very difficult to tell you which was the best and which may be the best in 1979.

'In my own mind I believe that a colt called Borzoi (by Round Table) is the best. He won the Exeter Stakes on the July course here and did not run again. He could easily be my number one for 1979 although he may not stay well enough to be a Derby colt.

'Main Reef, a very useful and dour sort of a horse, Lyphard's Wish (he could be anything on soft ground), R. B. Chesne, Golden River and Elysee Palace (which only ran once), are probably the best of the other colts but I must warn you there are

17

several unknown quantities among the Wildenstein horses and at least a couple which according to Angel Penna could be outstanding.'

The fascinating point about his 1978 crop of two-year-olds is that when getting his yearlings together in 1977 he decided to concentrate on colts and not worry to buy fillies of which therefore he only had a few. Among this little band, however, were Formulate, Odeon and One in a Million, three of the top four or five of their sex.

Commenting on Gunner B's five wins Henry said : 'The horse improved after he came to me, probably because he had higher class horses to bring him along in his home work. This place is run on extravagant lines and I made a point of sending out Jim White—he has been with the stable for years—in a van every First Lot so that he could lead the colt on to the gallops on the Heath and elsewhere. Gunner B would not go near a canter unless Jim White was there.

'He is a great old character, that horse. You had to let him get away with almost everything. If you take their character away then they are no good anyway. He beat better horses than himself because he was so genuine.

'In 1978 we were a bit unlucky not to have done better with horses like Le Moss. He hated hard ground. He was just beaten in the St Leger by Julio Mariner. Le Moss kept changing his legs all the way up the straight. An hour's rain there and he would have won.'

The horse with which Henry had the most fun in 1976 was Buckskin, transferred from Peter Walwyn's string during the summer. Henry won the Doncaster and Jockey Club Cups with him.

'Nobody seems to want real stayers these days,' Henry said. 'We were offered only thirty thousand pounds for him. In my opinion that's insulting.

'I know he had a bad suspensory, but we took lots of X-rays and they showed that underneath the suspensory everything was clean and in fair order. I have decided to rest him until March next year (1979) and then train him for the Ascot Gold Cup. If I get him to Ascot then he will win. He is a very, very good horse.'

*   *   *

Thinking quietly on the subject of the help trainers' wives give their husbands these days, one has the impression that they are greater props and more active members of racing stable teams than say fifty or a hundred years ago. I think this is probably because women are prominent in more walks of life than when I was a boy and so the parts they play in most facets of racing are now fully evident. Having said this and having come, through my mother, from a family which bristles with the names of trainers and horse breeders, I can confirm that the majority of trainers' wives have always helped their men, albeit unobtrusively, in what is always an arduous and sometimes a very worrying profession. In times of dire trouble and grave emergency the trainer's wife of old rolled up her sleeves, hitched up her skirt and applied herself to the physical work demanded by the occasion. When smallpox swept through Newmarket many years ago, one of my ancestors who trained there found himself with forty horses and not a boy well enough to help carry on the routine. For several days, until help was available, that man and his wife fed, watered and mucked out those horses. I have no doubt that just the same was happening at other stables in the town.

There are of course many trainers' wives who today are out of the limelight but at the same time work hard and unobtrusively to keep the flag flying. Julie Cecil not only works hard at home but, like 'Bonk' Walwyn, Jean Jarvis and many other wives, figures in the public eye because she can, and does, ride work and at times acts as unlicensed assistant.

Julie is a good rider and thoroughly understands horses. 'She is a tremendous help to me in almost every branch of my job,' Henry told me. 'Julie pays more attention to detail than I do. She is more observant than I am. She is super with horses and I do not know what I would do without her. My view is that one simply has to have someone as a wife who understands horses, owners, and my job. I don't think I could be married to anybody who didn't. Apart from that I am a bit highly strung and Julie knows how to handle me!'

Well, that's a great tribute, and I have heard it expressed in one way or another by nearly every trainer lucky enough to have a devoted wife, fit for work!

Henry and Julie Cecil on the steps of Warren Place. (Brian Love)

Julie is also a wonderful mother. On one of my visits to Warren Place early in 1978 I had the pleasure of spending a happy hour with her and her two children, Katie, then six and a half, and Noel, just five. Both were charming and conversational.

As the little boy moved away from me across the wide drawing-room there was something very familiar about his walk. 'I know what you are thinking,' smiled Julie, 'he gets that, as well as his name, from his grandfather!'

'Of course,' I said, 'the action of his dam's sire!'

Well, that's racing for you.

STATISTICAL RECORDS

Henry Cecil has had (like Barry Hills) 10 seasons as a trainer. He has won 572 races on the Flat in Britain worth £1,313,272. He set a prize money record in 1978 with 109 winners of £382,812 in stakes, which just beat Peter Walwyn's 1975 record of £382,527 from 121 winners. He won 140 races up to the end of 1977 worth £1,000 or more to the winner, and in 1978 38 races worth more than £2,000 to the winner.

TRAINERS' TABLE

Year	Position	Winners	Stakes
1969	8th	29 winners of	£60,560
1971	10th	53 winners of	£52,354
1974	10th	50 winners of	£69,982
1975	2nd	82 winners of	£205,345
1976	1st	52 winners of	£261,301
1977	5th	74 winners of	£168,888
1978	1st	109 winners of	£382,812

BIG RACES

The races worth £4,000 or more to the winner were:

1969

ECLIPSE	Sandown	Wolver Hollow	£25,829
OBSERVER GOLD CUP	Doncaster	Approval	19,624

1971

MICHAEL SOBELL STAKES	Doncaster	Pert Lassie	6,465
MOLECOMB STAKES	Goodwood	Pert Lassie	5,122
CESAREWITCH	Newmarket	Orosio	8,385

1972

THE QUEEN'S VASE	Royal Ascot	Falkland	4,271

1974

JOCKEY CLUB STAKES	Newmarket	Relay Race	4,120
HARDWICKE STAKES	Royal Ascot	Relay Race	11,491
CHERRY HINTON STAKES	Newmarket	Roussalka	6,673
PETER HASTINGS STAKES	Newbury	One Night Stand	4,083

1975

TWO THOUSAND GUINEAS	Newmarket	Bolkonski	38,868
CECIL FRAIL HANDICAP	Haydock	Rebec	4,030
YELLOW PAGES	Sandown	Deerslayer	4,376
ST JAMES'S PALACE	Royal Ascot	Bolkonski	9,615
CORONATION STAKES	Royal Ascot	Roussalka	9,923
OLD NEWTON CUP	Haydock	Fool's Mate	4,330
SUSSEX STAKES	Goodwood	Bolkonski	18,275

NASSAU STAKES	Goodwood	Roussalka	£10,720
LAURENT PERRIER CHAMPAGNE	Doncaster	Wollow	8,593
WM HILL DEWHURST	Newmarket	Wollow	23,189
OBSERVER GOLD CUP	Doncaster	Take Your Pick	26,003

1976

CLERICAL MEDICAL GREENHAM	Newbury	Wollow	6,308
TWO THOUSAND GUINEAS	Newmarket	Wollow	49,581
DEE STAKES	Chester	Great Idea	4,807
RIBBLESDALE STAKES	Royal Ascot	Catalpa	17,555
THE QUEEN'S VASE	Royal Ascot	General Ironside	6,514
SUSSEX STAKES	Goodwood	Wollow	31,639
PTS LAURELS	Goodwood	Fool's Mate	7,839
NASSAU STAKES	Goodwood	Roussalka	13,092
BENSON AND HEDGES GOLD CUP	York	Wollow	40,402
ECLIPSE	Sandown	Wollow	38,258

1977

WESTBURY STAKES	Sandown	Lucky Wednesday	7,132
DEE STAKES	Chester	Royal Plume	6,139
CECIL FRAIL	Haydock	Owen Jones	8,988
SANYO	Epsom	Amboise	4,157
PRINCE OF WALES	Royal Ascot	Lucky Wednesday	13,272
MORLAND BREWERY	Newbury	Royal Hive	5,286
WILLIAM HILL GOLD CUP	Redcar	Aliante	9,435
VIRGINA	Newcastle	Miss Pinkie	7,225
PARKHILL	Doncaster	Royal Hive	12,662

1978

EARL OF SEFTON	Newmarket	Gunner B	11,050
PRINCESS ELIZABETH	Epsom	Varishkina	6,662
BRIGADIER GERARD	Sandown	Gunner B	9,448
DIOMED	Epsom	Ovac (ITY)	10,976
HERMES	Epsom	Water Frolic	7,041
PRINCE OF WALES	Royal Ascot	Gunner B	15,986
QUEEN'S VASE	Royal Ascot	Le Moss	6,810
CHESHAM	Royal Ascot	Main Reef	6,243
JOE CORAL ECLIPSE	Sandown	Gunner B	42,414
JULY STAKES	Newmarket	Main Reef	15,514
BLUE SEAL	Ascot	One in a Million	4,064
TENNENT TROPHY	Ayr	Le Moss	8,491
HUNGERFORD	Newbury	Tannenberg (USA)	10,172
WATERFORD CANDELABRA	Goodwood	Formulate	4,744
MARCH	Goodwood	Le Moss	4,526
INTERCROFT SOLARIO	Sandown	Lyphard's Wish	4,721
LAURENT PERRIER	Doncaster	R. B. Chesne	17,105
DONCASTER CUP	Doncaster	Buckskin (FR)	10,299

VALDOE	Goodwood	Gunner B	£6,287
HOOVER FILLIES MILE	Ascot	Formulate	11,806
JOCKEY CLUB CUP	Newmarket	Buckskin (FR)	11,220
HOUGHTON	Newmarket	One in a Million	4,571
HORRIS HILL	Newbury	Kris	15,759

BEST RACECOURSES

Newmarket	91	wins
Yarmouth	63	,,
Goodwood	33	,,
Nottingham	32	,,
Doncaster	28	,,
Warwick	24	,,
Ascot	23	,,
Newbury	21	,,
Sandown	19	,,
Leicester	19	,,

JOCKEYS

Joe Mercer	146	wins
Greville Starkey	137	,,
Alan Bond	72	,,
Lester Piggott	66	,,
Frank Durr	31	,,
G. Dettori	18	,,

Bill O'Gorman, Philip Mitchell, Franca Vittadini and Suzanne Kane are among amateurs who have ridden winners for Cecil.

BEST MONTHS

July	138	wins
August	89	,,
September	81	,,
May	76	,,
June	69	,,

No races won in March '78.

MULTIPLE WINS

He had 73 doubles, 17 trebles, one four-timer, and a five-timer on 22nd July 1978, a double at Newmarket and a treble at Warwick. Eight doubles at Newmarket (straight), and six trebles at Newmarket (straight), plus five doubles with one leg at Newmarket, and two trebles, a four-timer and a five-timer involving Newmarket. He has had seven straight doubles at Yarmouth, plus three mixed doubles with Yarmouth, two straight trebles, and one mixed treble with Yarmouth.

OWNERS

Cecil has had approximately 90 winning owners. The late Sir Humphrey de Trafford, Mrs John Hanes, Mr Charles St George and family, Mrs Stanhope Joel, Sir Reginald Macdonald Buchanand and family, Lord Howard de Walden, Mr H. J. Joel, Count D'Alessio and Mr Marcus Wickham Boynton are or have been among his stalwart supporters.

FIRST WINNERS TRAINED

Celestial Cloud, Ripon, Newby Amateur Stakes. Owner Mrs Cecil, ridden by Bill O'Gorman, on 17th May 1969.

HORSES

Pride of Alcide won in '69, '70, '71. Irvine won in '71, '72, '73. Roussalka won in '74, '75, '76. Albrighton won in '74, '75, '76. Arisaig in '71, '72, '73, '74 and Fool's Mate in '74, '75, '76, '77 and '78.

RACES FARMED

OBSERVER GOLD CUP, Doncaster	1969, 1975
TWO THOUSAND GUINEAS, Newmarket	1975, 1976
SUSSEX STAKES, Goodwood	1975, 1976
ECLIPSE, Sandown	1969, 1976, 1978
QUEEN'S VASE, Ascot	1972, 1976, 1978
NASSAU STAKES, Goodwood	1975, 1976
LAND O' BURNS, Ayr	1970, 1972
TRUNDLE STAKES, Goodwood	1973, 1975, 1976
DARLEY BREWERY STAKES, Pontefract	1974, 1976, 1977
LAURENT PERRIER CHAMPAGNE, Doncaster	1975, 1978
PRINCE OF WALES, Royal Ascot	1977, 1978

TWO-YEAR-OLD WINNERS

For three of the past four years Cecil's first two-year-old winner of the season has been at Yarmouth at the end of May meeting.

GENERAL

1978 was notable, not only for his excellent two-year-olds, but for the number of wins at very short prices with maidens, especially at Yarmouth. Frassino won the Gran Premio Citta di Napoli (£8,685) on 16th July. Main Reef passed the post first in the Mill Reef Stakes at Newbury but was disqualified and placed second. Le Moss was second in the St Leger.

John Dunlop

of Arundel

Until Shirley Heights won the Derby and the Irish Sweeps Derby in 1978, the highlight of Arundel trainer John Dunlop's career was the victory of the Duke of Norfolk's Ragstone, in the 1974 Ascot Gold Cup.

The reason for this, which will be obvious to many, is that for years the Duke was Her Majesty the Queen's Representative at Ascot. He was also the architect of modern Ascot.

Before we look at how John became a trainer, let him tell the Ragstone story as he recounted it to me at his home on a spur of the South Downs above the historic Sussex town of Arundel.

'Ascot,' said John, 'was to the Duke the most important race-course in the country and therefore the Gold Cup was one of the races he really wanted to win. I don't think he had ever had a runner in the race before.

'Ragstone, who was by Ragusa, out of Fotheringay, by Right Royal, ran once as a two-year-old, at Windsor, in September 1972. Then in the spring when he was a three-year-old he had some minor shoulder problem. He did not run until the end of July when he won first time out at Newbury. Next he won a little race at Windsor. Then we sent him up to Ayr and he won again. After that we went to Newmarket in October for a very competitive mile-and-a half event, the Southfield Handicap. Piggott rode him carrying 9 st 7 lb. He won, not all that impressively, but he won.

'He had shown enough to encourage us to decide to make a Gold Cup horse of him as a four-year-old but in fact I think his best distance was a mile and a half or a mile and six furlongs. He was

Ragstone, centre, ridden by Ron Hutchinson, winning the Ascot Gold Cup from Proverb (Willie Carson) on the right, with Lassalle (Lester Piggott), third. (Sport & General)

a very high class horse but a puller. He was not a natural slogging stayer type that wins races by stamina plus a bit of speed such as Alycidon and Sagaro. His first wins as a four-year-old were the Aston Park Stakes (1 m 5 f) at Newbury and the Henry II Stakes (2 m) at Sandown.

'Then he won a really good Gold Cup. He beat Proverb, a top class horse, winner of the Goodwood Cup in 1973 and 1974, and the Doncaster Cup (1974). Ragstone won this race with class and authority. He came from behind and finished with a great turn of foot. That was the most marvellous day for the late Duke because the reception afterwards—I have never heard anything like it at Ascot—was fantastic.'

I remember the scene well. Everybody, including the losers, seemed so thrilled. We had laughter and tears, it was so emotional. John said, 'We all went to the Royal Box—it was terrific. We had aimed at this for five months and could hardly believe it had happened. Usually these long-laid plans go awry.

'We had bought a little horse called Hornet from Peter Walwyn to make the running. Tommy Carter was on him and, of course, Ron Hutchinson was on Ragstone. Tommy rode Hornet beautifully. The horse was not in the race to make a strong gallop. As I have said already Ragstone was really a mile-and-a-half horse and a hard puller. Tommy had to make the running fast enough for our horse to settle just behind him but steady enough not to make it too much of a test of stamina.'

Alec Head ran a high class horse, Authi, half-brother to Hard to Beat, with a pacemaker, Fire Bug. So there were two pacemakers in the race. Jallu set off at a brisk pace on Fire Bug. All the way up that long straight which is the Hunt Cup Mile, the first part of the Gold Cup course, Tommy Carter was calling to Jallu that he was going too fast and ought to steady down. Jallu eventually took the hint and hauled back to be just in front of Hornet. So Tommy, although not in front, can be said to have dictated the pace. He did the job to perfection but it was a worrying process for the Arundel party! Another member of the field was Lassalle, winner of the 1973 Gold Cup, with a brilliant burst of speed. This time Lester Piggott shot the horse into the lead on the turn for home, but he failed to hold off Ragstone's and Proverb's finishing bursts.

'We then planned to bring Ragstone back to one and a half miles and run him in the Arc de Triomphe,' said John, 'but he injured himself in the Geoffrey Freer Stakes at Newbury in heavy ground and that was the end of his racing career.'

Most unhappily for all concerned with Ragstone, he had to be put down in August 1978 when he fractured his skull in a fall at the Lavington Stud, Graffham, in Sussex. One of his first crop to race, Muneca, won a seven-furlong nursery at Wolverhampton just after Ragstone's death.

27

*   *   *

John Leeper Dunlop was born on 10th July 1939, in Tetbury, Gloucestershire, son of a country doctor, a founder member of Chepstow racecourse.

He is an Ulsterman by descent. His tall slim figure, sandy hair and lean face give him the look of an eagle. In fact if we go beyond the Ulsterman I wouldn't mind betting that one of his distant ancestors was a Norseman who voyaged hazardously round the north coast of Scotland eventually to settle in the West.

The impression I have of him is that he was destined for horse racing from an early age. As so often happens it took a mother's prodding to stir him into earning a living. Once started he put his heart and soul into the racing game. That, plus the luck of which there is more than one example in his life, notably of being at the right place at the right time, landed him as trainer to the Duke and Duchess of Norfolk at Arundel in 1965.

John's father practised in Herefordshire, then in Tetbury and returned to Hereford in 1947. Not only was he a founder member of Chepstow but an enthusiastic member of Cheltenham. No wonder young John went racing as a child. He recalls those days: 'I took a photograph of Gordon Richards in racing silks on the Chepstow weighing room steps. He was very kind and let me take it. Awful cheek on my part.'

That was not the end of the matter for at the next meeting John took the photograph with him and asked Gordon to autograph it, which he did. I would not call this cheek, but the action of an enterprising child.

Eventually he went into the Army for his National Service and joined the Royal Ulster Rifles. 'When I'd finished with the R.U.R. I decided I was going to try racing as a career,' he said. 'I had one or two vague racing connections but no immediate entrée in any possible way. Like so many other youngsters at that time I was kicking around at home doing nothing. After several months of this my mother said, "Now come on. What are you going to do?".'

So he put an advertisement in the *Sporting Life* something like this: 'Young man, mad about racing, keen, but no practical experience. Prepared to do anything. Money immaterial.' 'It really is quite amusing looking back at the lordly way I worded this because I had no private means or virtually none,' he commented.

He got about ten replies from all sorts of people including Arthur Budgett, trainer of two Derby winners and about whom Bill Curling has written such an informative book, *Derby Double* (William Luscombe).

Eventually John, having sifted the answers to his advertisement, phoned Neville Dent who trained at Brockenhurst in the New Forest and would later stand the successful stallion Comedy Star at his Hart Hill Stud. He had a string of about fifteen or twenty jumpers and 'sounded nice and friendly' so he went there. John lived in a caravan near the yard and worked for virtually nothing.

'I looked after two, sometimes three or four horses, and a premium stallion. I drove the horse box. I travelled the horses and did a bit of everything for about two years. This was great fun and I loved it.

'This, for me, was a very good experience because, as I say, I had to do everything which would not have been the case in a big yard such as Budgett's. Not only did I enjoy it from the racing point of view but from the breeding aspect as well. We journeyed Neville's stallions all over the place, covering all sorts of extraordinary mares, carthorses, New Forest ponies and the occasional thoroughbred.'

Then after two years in this happy, carefree job the *Sporting Life* again played its part in fashioning John's career. He was looking at this newspaper at breakfast and read that Gordon Smyth, who trained for the Duke and Duchess of Norfolk and others at Arundel, was seeking an assistant cum secretary. John rang up Gordon, having noticed that he had a runner at Salisbury that day and said that he could be at the races and would like to meet him with a view to having a chance of the job. Gordon agreed so off went John to Salisbury and was, in due course, hired.

Not for the first time did a young man say that he could do all that was required of him when in fact he was not being strictly accurate. It was a gamble that came off as John told me: 'Gordon said that I was to do all the secretarial work, PAYE, accounts, typing letters and everything else. I said breezily "Oh yes. No problem". In fact I had never tapped a typewriter or written a

Sue and John Dunlop at home with Timothy (left), Harry and Edward.

business letter in my life. I hadn't got a clue. I didn't even know what PAYE stood for, let alone how to do it. Shortly after that someone in a pub told me how. I had a couple of typing lessons and I told myself "I'll get by".' He did.

So John came to Arundel and literally did do all the secretarial work. The stable was not as big as it is now. There were only about thirty or forty horses. John recalled: 'Even so there was plenty to do and, as Gordon had promised, I did my assistant bit and went racing quite a lot. I had plenty to do with the horses and I got on well with the head lad. That was fortunate for it is an essential ingredient of a happy yard.'

Just as the Dunlop ship was sailing happily along it went aground. John became very ill. He was struck down by an obscure chest ailment. He had four months in King Edward VII's Hospital, Midhurst, during the latter half of the second season he was at Arundel.

30

When he came out, with no health problems, he returned to work and learned that Gordon Smyth was thinking of moving to Lewes. Much to John's surprise and delight he was asked if he would like to take over the trainer's licence at Arundel.

He was only twenty-seven, just married and poised for a new and thrilling phase in his life.

In June of 1965 he had married Sue, daughter of Gerard T. Page. John and Sue now have three sons, Timothy John Leeper, Edward Alexander Leeper and Harry James Leeper, who share their father's keen interest in many aspects of country life and games. Evidence of enthusiasm for cricket at House on the Hill, Arundel, is a single-wicket pitch from which stumps are rarely drawn in the summer holidays. I suspect that, when available, John senior is put on to bowl some lengthy overs. There was more evidence of the family's devotion to games when I called one day to see John. 'Sorry,' he said, 'Sue is not here. She has gone to see the boys play in a Fives match.' So what with husband, horses, sons and owners, Sue Dunlop is, like most trainers' wives, fully extended!

We next turned to training at Arundel: 'All the working ground at Arundel is uphill with the result, I think, that it has a beneficial effect. You don't have to go so fast to achieve the same work-rate as on flat, fast ground. If a horse needs "x" amount of work to get it fit you can do that in a shorter time, and probably at a slower rate at Arundel than, shall we say, Newmarket. That is important because in most cases it is speed that causes injuries. When it comes to trying horses here at Arundel,' John continued, 'it is almost impossible. The gallops are stiff and if you try to work horses flat out it is not successful. You can simulate race conditions more easily on Newmarket Heath than at Arundel if you want to have a shrewd idea of what is going to happen on the course. One does find at Arundel that one turns up occasionally with long-priced winners because the horses are not tried before a race. We run them in the hope that they will go well.' In this I don't think John is being entirely fair to himself as a successful trainer. He does nearly always have a sound idea about the ability and fitness of a horse, but the point he makes about dress rehearsals is understandable.

'At Newmarket on the racecourse side of the Heath, there is a stiff and slightly steep gallop where you can tell how fit a horse is and assess his ability pretty thoroughly but I seldom work a horse at home more than six furlongs whether it is a sprinter or a two-mile horse,' John went on. 'The late Duke of Norfolk's Ragstone won the Ascot Gold Cup of two and a half miles but we never worked him more than six furlongs at home. This method sometimes leads you astray. When you are not working at racing pace you can have some marvellous three-quarter speed horses that seem to be potential world beaters. Yes, fine at three-parts pace, but when they get on the racecourse one asks oneself where the hell the other part has gone? In fact they haven't got another gear.

'It can be said that I err on the side of being an easy trainer rather than a hard one. That suits my methods or to put it another way my methods have become adjusted to the ground on which I have been working my horses.'

John's remarks about training methods at Arundel prompt one to consider how it became a training centre. The Dukes of Norfolk owned a racing stable called Michelgrove where Victor Gilpin trained before World War II. Michelgrove is on the South Downs about a mile and a half north-east of Patching. It was usually let and was not a private stable. John Hislop, one time leading amateur rider, now a breeder, author and expert on racing affairs, was with the trainer Victor Gilpin when he moved from Clarehaven, Newmarket, to Michelgrove in 1935. At that time the Duke, Bernard Norfolk, had several horses with Gilpin. The number was increased after the Duke had married because the Duchess was a great racing enthusiast and has been ever since. There were however never more than eight or ten Norfolk horses at Michelgrove.

When Victor Gilpin and John Hislop went to Michelgrove it was at the suggestion of the Duke of Norfolk. The stables and gallops had not been used by a string of thoroughbreds since before World War I when Davies Scourfield sent out Perola to win the Oaks from this glorious place in 1909, the year King Edward VII

A smiling John Dunlop at the start of the 1978 season, in which he won two Derbys with Shirley Heights.

won the Derby with Minoru. The King very nearly landed the great Epsom double that year. His Princesse de Galles was a two length runner-up to Perola which was sired by Persimmon, winner of the Derby and St Leger in the Royal colours in 1896 when His Majesty was Prince of Wales.

Anyone who has lived and worked among the South Downs above the teeming coast must be conversant with their charm. The essays of Hilaire Belloc alerted me as a schoolboy to their beauty and John Hislop's description of training horses at Michelgrove in *Far from a Gentleman* (Michael Joseph, 1960) increases the nostalgia.

Early in World War II the Army took over the Michelgrove downland as a tank training ground. The first unit there did its best not to ruin the gallops. There was plenty of room for tank training without badly interfering with the narrow strips on which the horses worked. The next unit that appeared at Michelgrove was not so obliging. They were politely asked if they would drive their tanks in a way that would spare the actual gallops from unnecessary punishment. I am reliably informed that this unit didn't think this was very funny in the middle of a war and the outcome was that they mutilated most of the turf with U turns and other damaging manoeuvres. That was the end of the gallops.

The Duke and Duchess then decided to give up Michelgrove as a training stable. It was a great disappointment to them, but they were not beaten. The Duchess had the idea of bringing the horses to Arundel. The Castle grounds consisted then of 'a park full of trees' as John Dunlop put it. There was also the carriage horse yard, consisting of about a dozen boxes plus coach and carriage houses. It was a bold step to contemplate but they decided to go ahead. I should say at this point that racehorses had been trained on the Downs at Arundel at various times during the past three or more centuries but not it would seem where the new gallops were made.

Anyone who would help during the last years of the war and immediately afterwards was engaged in tree felling and ground levelling, arduous tasks in which both the Duke and Duchess participated. Thus were made the gallops that exist now.

There was a big block of wooden boxes at Michelgrove. Somehow they were lifted up more or less in one piece and transported to Arundel. So, with old boxes and new gallops, training was resumed at Arundel shortly after the war with Willy Smyth in charge. Eventually his son Gordon took over and in the course of time John succeeded Gordon.

John reminded me that this important move was all done on the spur of the moment in the war years and that the establishment has been built up and improved ever since. 'There is room now for a hundred horses,' John said. 'When everything is "in" the number in my string hovers somewhere between eighty and the century.'

'The gallops when I came here first were very good. They had been treated and manicured. We put down a sand canter and since then have made two wood shavings gallops which are invaluable. Training a big string of horses as I do, I don't know how I would get on without them because the amount of grass is limited.

'One of the great things about Newmarket is that any day of the year there is always somewhere to work your horses and you are not responsible for its maintenance,' said John with some feeling!

Now let's have a look at what goes into the Arundel boxes. Almost all the Norfolk horses are homebred. The Earl and Countess of Halifax, owners of Shirley Heights, also send yearlings of their own breeding. So do Roderick More O'Farrell and Daniel Prenn. There are several other small owner-breeders who keep a mare or two at home and have a few animals in training at the same time.

'We buy quite a few horses at auction each year. The British Bloodstock Agency has clients in the stable, so have the Anglo-Irish Bloodstock Agency, the Curragh Bloodstock Agency and the Newmarket Bloodstock Agency, and two or three other agencies. I personally choose a few horses for my patrons with mixed success.' I doubt whether any trainer can say much better than that.

I asked John if he, when buying or selecting a horse for his stable, is chiefly influenced by appearance or does he put pedigree first?

'I buy primarily on looks,' he replied. 'Because I have very few owners who can match the purchasing power of those who buy only horses with high class pedigrees. A good-looking horse with a top pedigree now fetches an astronomical price. The one chance I have got in the open market is to buy an attractive individual. And don't forget that the great majority of horses are relatively well bred.'

When John goes to a sale he likes to look for an animal which in his opinion will make a stayer rather than a sprinter. 'I like to have horses that can stay a mile and a quarter and even a little further because at those distances we find the most valuable prize money anywhere in the world.

'It is very hard to win with sprinting two-year-olds, in fact the sprints are a very competitive area in which to run horses. If we leave out horses with classic pedigrees the yearling that looks like being a sprinter is usually more expensive than the others. For the same money you can usually buy a nicer horse that stays than you can a sprinter.

'Another factor is that if you have a mile-and-a-quarter horse that can win his maiden race he then has a certain amount of value to go jumping. And that value has increased in recent years owing to the wider interest in, and larger prize money for, the winter game.'

As the racing enthusiast will have surmised John does not have a stable full of precocious two-year-olds, and he does not have to bustle up the youngsters before they are ready for it.

'I have always had marvellous owners, particularly the Duchess —and of course the Duke when he was alive,' John enthused. 'They leave me alone to do what I consider is right for the horses. Luckily for me most of my owners think along the same lines as I do. That's why I have virtually a free hand. I haven't got any owners who want results in five minutes.' However, I feel sure that if John, through the changing circumstances of racing economics, had to produce early winners then he is sufficiently professional to cope successfully. In fact the record book proves that he can do this if required. What about Cagnes-sur-Mer? He had half a dozen winners there in February and March 1978. Winners and place money brought in £24,000.

*   *   *

Like so many of the leading trainers I have met, John says he has
been very lucky in the matter of staff. I believe this but one finds
that the majority of top trainers are good managers of men.
When John started at Arundel he had a head lad called Dennis
Hartigan who, not surprisingly, is an Irishman; a travelling head
man called Eddie Watt, a Scotsman; and the second head man is
a Welshman, Renfield Jenkins.

'They were going strong when I started and they are still
going strong, and I hope they will be for many more years. They
know by now what I like, what I do, and what I want to do,' said
John. 'The other person I should mention is Robert Baker who
has been with me for six or seven years as my professional
assistant. He has been invaluable. He started in a racing stable
with me, has ridden point-to-point winners and knows something
about farming. I'm sorry to say that he is now leaving me to join
Ryan Price.'

Turning to racecourses I reminded John that in the last twelve
years he had a good record at Newmarket although Newbury and
Brighton have brought him the most winners in that time.

'Well, Newmarket is the place to go. One has to,' he said.
'Of course there is wonderful racing there. Everyone knows that
and it is unnecessary to go on about it. You know already how I
feel about Ascot where Ragstone and other horses from Arundel
have had such memorable wins. Goodwood is also one of my
favourites, for obvious reasons. So is Sandown.'

Then came an unexpected switch. 'I find Wolverhampton not a
bad racecourse. It is quite a good course from the horses' point of
view, and all things considered a fine galloping track. I have had
plenty of winners there. The standard of competition is not too
high. It is hard to find a decent racecourse for the moderate horse.
When I say decent I mean one that does not have tight turns and
the horses do not have to gallop up and down hill. I would couple
Nottingham with Wolverhampton. I suppose I like them about
the best of the bread-and-butter courses.

'We send horses regularly to Ayr which is an excellent racecourse and has very good prize money. Ron Hutchinson would

Shirley Heights (G. Starkey) sticks his neck out to beat Exdirectory (C. Roche) by a head, with Hawaiian Sound (W. Shoemaker) third, in the Irish Sweeps Derby 1978.

always go to any of these courses to ride for us. Never ever has he, like some of the prima donnas we know, objected to riding anywhere. If in the midst of Royal Ascot I said to him, "I have got a runner at Lanark tomorrow. Do you mind going up there rather than ride here?" he would have said, "No, I will do whatever you wish."

'In fact Hutchie is a most marvellous man to have ridden for one. Firstly he is an extraordinarily good jockey, a wonderful judge of pace and a very nice man too. Secondly he was a loyal stable jockey who never tried to get off something to ride a horse for somebody else, and finally he has always been a good friend and help to the stable generally over so many years.'

*   *   *

John has a predilection for enterprising raids on foreign prizes. Is this his Viking blood? I've had the pleasure of meeting John and Susan in the south of France in the late winter. His comments on these trips I found fascinating : 'It's a long winter without much excitement for everybody in a flat-racing stable. The prize money at Cagnes-sur-Mer is very good, and if you can find the right horses these expeditions can be very profitable. We proved this the first two years we went down there. Since then the competition has hotted up, thanks largely to Charlie Millbanks who takes some of his best horses down there. I have been leading trainer there twice. When we won the Grand Prix at Cagnes with My Brief we sold him for a lot of money. We have also won plenty of races in Belgium.'

John starts to prepare his Cagnes runners in early January, even sometimes before Christmas. They are shipped down in two hops by road. They stay the first night at Fontainebleau, near Paris, and polish off the rest of the journey the next day.

When the horses are run the first time they are probably three-parts or even seven-eighths fit. 'This does not sound an expert thing to do,' admitted John, 'but it is unavoidable really. You can't get horses completely fit training them down there. So they go down fit enough to run and once the racing has got them in top gear, well, from then on it's easy enough to keep them ticking over.

'I find the trip to Cagnes is beneficial rather than otherwise. The horses come back ready for the Kempton Easter meeting or some other meeting of reasonable quality. Belper, who as you know has one eye, won the City and Suburban at Epsom, having been to Cagnes where he won an Amateur Riders Race ridden by Robert Baker.

'We have won races in Germany. Burglar won at Hamburg. Funny Man won the Grand Prize at Gelsenkirchen in 1975. North Stoke scored at Baden Baden last year (1977). We have won a lot of races in Belgium and at least a dozen in Ostend in one year. We took the Grand Prix in Brussels in 1977 with North Stoke, in fact we have won races at all the Belgium tracks.'

He sends only a few horses to Deauville so it is not surprising that a winner there has escaped him so far.

His adventurous spirit has received few setbacks, although he does classify one expedition with six fillies to Naples as 'rather a disastrous performance. The idea was that we bought them specially for the job of racing and selling them in Italy. It was great sport actually and the horses made a gross profit, but the costs were very high, and they took two years or more to pay us the stake money.'

In 1970 John sent Black Satin over to Ireland to win the One Thousand Guineas. Before that she had been third in the Cheveley Park Stakes and third in the English One Thousand Guineas behind Humble Duty. She was by Linacre. Her half sister, Front Row, trained by Ryan Jarvis, also won the Irish Guineas in 1968.

I sensed that after Ragstone John had considerable admiration for Scottish Rifle. He told me, 'Scottish Rifle is owned by a very good friend and a marvellous owner—Sandy Struthers who lives outside Glasgow. He has had numerous successes with not only Scottish Rifle but with Pitcairn, John Splendid and Mount Athos, third in the 1968 Derby to Sir Ivor.

'Scottish Rifle was one of the nicest horses I have ever trained. He had a charming temperament and was one of those rare horses which the vet never saw the entire time he was in training. He was runner up to Steel Pulse in the Irish Derby and won the Gordon Stakes at Goodwood. Next season he won the Eclipse but he was a disappointment in the Champion Stakes in which he was ridden by Lester Piggott who said the colt was "gone". In my opinion Piggott rode a moderate race on him. We then took him to America for the Washington International. He ran a super race and was third to that great filly Dahlia.'

As I write this book there are three horses which are much in John's mind. They are the six-year-old Balmerino from New Zealand, North Stoke, a four-year-old which cost 820 guineas as a yearling, and, of course, Shirley Heights.

Balmerino, owned by a New Zealand dairy farmer, Mr Ralph Stuart, is a bay by Trictrac, out of Dulcie, by Duccio. He was a top performer in New Zealand. Mr Stuart realised that the horse was so talented that it would be worthwhile campaigning him against the best opposition in Europe and America.

John Dunlop now takes up the story: 'I think Balmerino came to me originally because of Pat Samuel who has horses such as Grand Canyon with Derek Kent at Funtingdon, near Chichester. I trained the odd horse for him on the Flat. He rang me up sometime during the winter of 1976–7 and asked me if I would take Balmerino. I said I'd be interested. To be honest I didn't really know much about him. The implication was that the horse would come over with his trainer and they wanted somewhere for him to stay. At the end of it all I said I would be delighted to help them.

'Pat Samuel added that the horse was about to go to California to race and that after that they would like to bring him to England. Well, that was fine but one has so many of this type of request and often they do not come to anything. So I was pleasantly surprised when Ralph Stuart rang me up in June from California and said he definitely wanted to send the horse to England and would I take him?'

John agreed and Balmerino arrived at the end of July 1977. The objective was to run him in the Arc de Triomphe and, hopefully, to win it. The horse arrived at Arundel having run four times in California. He was flown over almost immediately after his fourth outing there, having won one small overnight entry race.

By the time he got to Sussex in the first week in August he was in a sorry state. He had run disappointingly in the three main races which were the purpose of his trip in America. In John's words 'Balmerino was pretty generally debilitated'. The trainer obviously had a problem because as the horse had run up light it was very necessary to build him up again. It was also desirable to race him once or twice so that both trainer and jockey could learn something about the horse in order that he could be ridden the right way in the big Longchamp race. Really John wanted to take Balmerino along quietly for six weeks or more and then get him ready for the Arc. That was impossible because this race was in the first week in October and that left the trainer with only two months. To his great credit he achieved almost all he set out to do and produced Balmerino fit to run for his life at Longchamp on Sunday, 2nd October.

Now let John come in again: 'We only had four races in the two months in which we could run him. We planned to run him in

41

Greville Starkey and Balmerino going out to run in the Clive Graham Stakes at Goodwood in May 1978, which he won.

the Valdoe Stakes at Goodwood and then the Cumberland Lodge Stakes at Ascot. If he ran well enough in those two races then he would go for the Arc. He was a difficult horse to train because he was so light after his Californian campaign. Well, I had to make the best of it. We had no option.

'He is a lovely mover—the best you ever saw—and a charming, sound horse. In fact he is a most attractive horse in every way.

'I got him ready quietly and rather half heartedly to run at Goodwood. However he did go extremely well in his last couple of bits of work before the Valdoe Stakes. I realised then that he was a pretty good horse. This was fully confirmed when he won so very easily by five lengths from Lucent, a top second-class filly. All the pundits were very impressed. Balmerino at once entered the Arc betting at third or fourth favourite.'

That was most satisfactory for Balmerino's supporters but John's anxiety about the horse had not been completely swept from his mind. He wanted to run him, once more, in his planned Ascot engagement so that he and Hutchinson could learn a bit more about the horse. The snag was that Balmerino had not taken his Goodwood race well. He had lost more weight than he should have done and it seemed to have got him keyed up mentally.

'That was funny,' explained John, 'because Goodwood is only a very short trip away from Arundel. From the moment he left our yard to his arrival home after the race he was away about four hours or only a few minutes more. Don't forget that he also won very easily.'

So John decided to give the Cumberland Lodge Stakes a miss and run the horse next in the Arc. There he acquitted himself wonderfully well, coming with a strong burst to beat all but the Lester Piggott ridden Alleged, winner by one and a half lengths.

John Dunlop's view on this race was that Balmerino was possibly a little unlucky not to win. He told me, 'It was not Balmerino's fault. It was not Hutchinson's fault. It could have been the extraordinary circumstance under which the race was run in that they went no gallop. The Arc is usually run at a cracking gallop all the way and there are often two or three pacemakers. Piggott was allowed to make much of the running on Alleged which he did in a comparatively leisurely fashion. This suited him but not our horse. If there had been a stronger gallop Balmerino would have got much nearer to Alleged. It was a most odd Arc!'

Be that as it may this £140,845 international mile-and-a-half race was one more example of how Lester Piggott, because of his skill, personality and reputation, can often mesmerize his opponents, as a stoat does a rabbit.

Balmerino's connections had high hopes for him in 1978 but the colt began to show signs of wear, possibly as a result of travelling and campaigning. He won the Clive Graham Stakes at Goodwood was runner-up to Crow in the Coronation Cup and to Gunner B in the Joe Coral Eclipse Stakes. He was slightly disappointing in other high class races. 'There is no doubt that he lacked real enthusiasm and towards mid-summer he began to deteriorate,' was John's summing up. The colt was sent back to New Zealand after a brave sortie in the Northern Hemisphere and one that enriched the racing scene.

Mrs Marcel Lequime's North Stoke, by Northfields (USA) out of Mother, by Whistler, was bred by the Ongar Stud and bought by the Newmarket Bloodstock Agency for only 820 guineas. What a bargain! By the end of his three-year-old career he had won eight races worth £56,872.87p.

North Stoke won twice over seven furlongs as a two-year-old. He won second time out as a three-year-old and took his next five races 'off the reel'. The average of his winning distances in 1977 was about six and a half lengths.

The colt won all his races so easily, it was, as John remarked, 'unbelievable'.

He completed his winning run in the Joe MacGrath Memorial Stakes (£19,624) at Leopardstown, a Group 1 race, by eight lengths which is a long way in a top class race. Next, in October, came the Champion Stakes. 'I know,' said John, 'that many people thought he ran a good race, finishing a fair third to Flying Water and Relkino, but he disappointed me. In fact in my opinion he didn't run his race at all. It was not his form. I think there was a combination of troubles. I believe that the travelling had caught up with him. He had a setback after he got home from Ireland and was sick for a few days. I admit that when he went off to Newmarket for the Champion I thought he was all right but the race proved that he was not. The ground was firm and this plus the fact that it was a falsely run race enabled the French filly to produce a tremendous finish. Nothing was right for him that day and I am adamant that he is a better horse than that form.'

It seems that when John first began to train North Stoke it was almost impossible to imagine that he might be a good horse. He was very lazy and idle. He would work with anything and was un-impressive as indeed he was to look at, being leggy and immature.

*   *   *

Now for Lord Halifax's Shirley Heights, a bay colt by Mill Reef out of Hardiemma, by Hardicanute, and bred by Lord Halifax and his son Lord Irwin. He won a nice race at Newmarket early on in 1977 and wound up the season by reversing Sandown's Solario Stakes form with Bolak in Ascot's Royal Lodge Stakes (£10,365) 7 f, in September.

About a week before the Solario Stakes which was Shirley Heights' main target John was in Ireland at the sales. Robert Baker, his assistant, phoned John and told him that he was worried about Shirley Heights as he had got 'a bit of a leg'. John told Robert 'Don't do anything until I get home. Just leave him in his box.'

'I got back. There was a place—a bang on the tendon of his off fore—that had been worrying me for some weeks. Anyway the vet saw him and we decided it was all right to run him but he missed four days' exercise. We gave him one bit of work and then it came up absolutely bottomless ground—like a quagmire.'

John would not have run the colt but for the fact that Lord and Lady Halifax were on their way down from Yorkshire to see him run. They were greeted by their trainer in the car park with 'I really hate to run this horse. I'm not particularly worried about the leg but he is short of work. The ground is bad. Everything is wrong for him.'

The Halifaxes' reply was 'let him run'. John agreed but made the proviso that Hutchinson might have to pull up the colt in the race and walk him home. So Shirley Heights ran in a half-cock situation: 'Win if you can but don't knock him about if the situation looks hopeless.'

'I think that if he had been straight he would have won,' John told me. 'As it happened I think he blew up. Hutchy had to check him slightly in the last two hundred yards. He lost his impetus and that was it.'

John believed firmly that Shirley Heights could be a good horse. The colt certainly gave substance to this when next time out with Greville Starkey in the saddle at Ascot he beat Bolak by three-quarters of a length. This time he was not short of work and the ground was fast.

In the autumn of 1978 I went again to Arundel to talk to John Dunlop about the colt's great career, sad to say curtailed by a leg

Hawaiian Sound, ridden by American Willy Shoemaker, leads the 1978 Derby field round Tattenham Corner. Between this point and the winning post Shirley Heights (arrowed) overhauled thirteen rivals. (Sport & General)

injury before the St Leger, which the Yorkshire-based Halifax family quite naturally wanted to win almost as much as the Derby.

'You remember the colt knocked a leg in his box before the '77 Solario Stakes. Although we ran him there and at Ascot, it really was something we had to treat. So we blistered him,' John told me.

After this, Shirley Heights stood in his box well into January and so missed a lot of steady work. To add to his trainer's problems, late winter and early spring in West Sussex were very wet. As a result the colt was still short of work when beaten ten lengths by Whitsted in Sandown's Classic Trial on 22nd April.

'I was quite pleased with him in the circumstances,' said John. 'We had planned to run him next in the Dante Stakes at the York May meeting but as he obviously needed another race we took him to Newmarket for the Heathorn Stakes in which he gave Ile de

46

Shirley Heights' (right) brilliant last furlong surge takes him to a head victory from Hawaiian Sound, with Remainder Man (T. Ives) third. (Sport & General)

Bourbon ten pounds and a short head beating. With the benefit of hindsight we can see what a good performance that was, because Ile de Bourbon later won the King George at Ascot.'

This additional race put the colt right for York where he won impressively. Briefly he was favourite for the Derby which John thought he would win although he believed the colt would not be suited by the track.

'Immediately after the Dante Stakes Greville Starkey told us that the colt would win the Derby,' said John. 'He was filled with enthusiasm and overflowing with that optimism jockeys so often show just after winning. So I asked him, "Will the colt act at Epsom?" because he was a long-striding horse and not a handy type.'

Starkey's reply to this was: 'No, and it doesn't matter if he does not come down the hill. He will beat them for speed up the straight.' Starkey was absolutely right.

When Derby day arrived Shirley Heights found Tattenham Hill a very serious problem. 'He fell down the hill,' was how John described the colt's performance at the trickiest stage of the race.

Starkey, to his eternal credit, did not panic but held his mount together and then in the straight got down to ride the race of his life. He switched to an opening on the inside of the leaders and drove the bay colt up to head the enterprisingly-ridden Hawaiian Sound at the winning post.

Next came the Irish Sweeps Derby, which was not according to the original plan of campaign. The Halifax family wanted to be sure that the colt would be a hundred per cent for the St Leger in September. His only race before this final classic was to be the Voltigeur Stakes at York, but Shirley Heights went back to Arundel so well, and had taken so little out of himself after the Derby, that John recommended that the horse should go for the Irish Sweeps Derby.

'At the Curragh we would meet nothing except the horses we had beaten in the Derby. I did not see why we should not beat them again, and more easily than at Epsom because the Irish course would suit him better. We took him over to the Curragh, early in the week so that I could work him there. He went very, very well—much more sharply than he did at home. He blew very hard and worried me to death. The horse had always been a lazy worker at home and he became lazier as the season went on.

'A lot went wrong in the actual race. They went off at a great pace and early on Shirley Heights had an awful job to keep his place. Then he ran wide into the straight with Exdirectory on his outside. I just don't know why he did it. To cap it all Greville Starkey got cramp in his legs, but of course we didn't know about that until later. Anyway we went through agonies on the stand and, as you know, the colt got up in the last few strides to beat Exdirectory by a head. I had thought he would win easily and was very surprised when he did not.'

Shirley Heights was rested for a month and then John got him going again so that the Voltigeur–St Leger campaign could be carried out. The colt had done three bits of work at home and he was in his normal lazy form so John took him to Goodwood to work there a week after the main Goodwood meeting. He worked well and blew and sweated a lot. That's when he damaged his leg.

John admits he really does not know for sure what happened: 'He was a difficult colt to train in some ways because at times he was rather a violent character. When he was walking round or grazing he would suddenly leap in the air and throw himself about. He fell over twice during the year—once, going up the drive from the walking ground, he whipped round and slipped up. Another time going out to work he crossed his legs and down he went. He was a terrifying horse in that respect. Rodney Boult, the boy who rode him, did a marvellous job. I felt very sorry for him during all those dramas. They must have put years on him.'

Before being worked at Goodwood the horse, on his way from the paddock to the racecourse, did one of his dreadful leaps and half-twisted and half-slipped behind. 'Whether that led to the trouble with his leg I don't know. But he was like that. He was a heavy horse too,' was John's final comment.

'We had a terrible week when Shirley Heights went wrong,' John continued. 'At about the same time as that tragedy we had news that Ragstone had fractured his skull when at exercise at stud. The telephone kept ringing as a result of all this so we pushed off to a pony show with our younger son. While we were there we were told that our eldest son at Pony Club camp had had a bad accident. It was all too dramatic for words. Glad to say he had only broken his nose.'

In retrospect, it was a good job that the Irish Sweeps Derby had been included in Shirley Heights's programme. 'We were so lucky in that we won two Derbys by such short distances. We could easily have lost them and we would have then been looking to the Leger as the one classic we were going to win. And of course we never got to Doncaster. So we must consider ourselves very fortunate,' said John. When we remind ourselves that the colt's two Derby wins grossed £171,497, the point becomes even clearer.

This courageous and well up-to-standard Derby winner was syndicated, and stands at Sandringham. Shirley Heights was a British-bred Derby winner, which gave immense gratification not only to his breeders but to thousands who, although realising that the top-class thoroughbred today is frequently internationally-bred, are thrilled when one comes from our home paddocks. Her Majesty the Queen is among those who have taken shares in Shirley Heights.

John's first thirteen years as a licensed trainer have been remarkably successful. Not only has he trained Derby winners and the winner of a Royal Ascot Gold Cup, but he has sent out runners from Arundel to win at many of Europe's leading racecourses. His reputation has travelled across the world. Proof of this is that Ogden Mills ('Dinny') Phipps, member of one of America's greatest racing families, shipped nine homebred yearlings of great potential to John at Arundel in November 1978. This could mark the beginning of a new and even more successful era for the Tetbury-born doctor's son who was once told by his mother to stop hanging about and to go out and find a job.

STATISTICAL RECORDS

John Dunlop has had 13 seasons as a trainer and has won 665 races in Britain totalling £810,698 prize money (winners only).

BIG RACES
The races worth £4,000 or more to the winner were:

1968

SCOTTISH AND NEWCASTLE BREWERIES	Newcastle	Mount Athos	£4,670
GORDON STAKES	Goodwood	Mount Athos	4,279
1970			
SCOTTISH AND NEWCASTLE BREWERIES	Newcastle	Arthur	5,038
AYR GOLD CUP	Ayr	John Splendid	5,239
1971			
PRINCESS OF WALES STAKES	Royal Ascot	Arthur	4,217

1972			
GORDON STAKES	Goodwood	Scottish Rifle	£4,370
1973			
EARL OF SEFTON STAKES	Newmarket	Scottish Rifle	4,325
STAR FILLIES STAKES	Kempton	Chilli Girl	5,521
ROYAL HUNT CUP	Royal Ascot	Camouflage	7,651
ECLIPSE	Sandown	Scottish Rifle	37,437
1974			
LADBROKE BLUE RIBAND	Epsom	Pitcairn	4,683
GOLD CUP	Royal Ascot	Ragstone	19,431
OLD NEWTON CUP	Haydock	Belper	4,135
GOODWOOD MILE	Goodwood	Pitcairn	4,321
1976			
TOTE FREE HANDICAP	Newmarket	Man of Harlech	6,787
X Y Z HANDICAP	Newcastle	Palatable	6,308
LADBROKE DERBY TRIAL	Lingfield	Norfolk Air	7,266
EBBISHAM	Epsom	Red Ruby	4,452
WM HILL SILVER JUBILEE	Newmarket	Trusted	5,879
JOE CORAL STAKES	Ayr	Trusted	4,792
MOLECOMB	Goodwood	Be Easy	6,929
GREAT WESTERN STAKES	Newbury	Palmerston	4,103
1977			
BASS CLUBMAN	Haydock	North Stoke	7,996
DOBSON PEACOCK HANDICAP	Newcastle	Trusted	4,878
MOLECOMB	Goodwood	Hatta	7,731
DOONSIDE CUP	Ayr	Norfolk Air	6,918
1978			
HEATHORN	Newmarket	Shirley Heights	4,900
CLIVE GRAHAM	Goodwood	Balmerino	5,678
THE DERBY STAKES	Epsom	Shirley Heights	98,410
BESSBOROUGH	Royal Ascot	Billion	5,001
HARVEY JONES MEMORIAL	Haydock	Celebrated	5,501
PRINCESS ROYAL	Royal Ascot	Trillionaire	7,348

Many winners overseas, notably Shirley Heights in the Irish Sweeps Derby (£71,672) in 1978 and Black Satin in Irish One Thousand Guineas in 1970. He has won races regularly at Cagnes-sur-Mer and scored six times there in 1978. Other 1978 winners abroad included Leopard's Rock and Hideaway at Ostend, Celebrated in Holland and Long John in Denmark.

BEST RACECOURSES
Newbury	44	wins
Brighton	42	,,
Goodwood	42	,,

Eight Flat-Racing Stables

Windsor	36 wins
Newmarket	35 ,,
Lingfield	32 ,,
Wolverhampton	32 ,,
Folkestone	32 ,,
Kempton	28 ,,
Sandown	27 ,,
Salisbury	26 ,,

JOCKEYS

Ron Hutchinson	432 wins (now retired)
Willie Carson	38 ,,
Lester Piggott	21 ,,
J. Ware	21 ,,
D. Gillespie	18 ,,
Richard Muddle	18 ,,

BEST MONTHS

July	151 wins
June	113 ,,
August	106 ,,
May	81 ,,
September	79 ,,

MULTIPLE WINS

John Dunlop had a four-timer in this country, plus the Irish Sweeps Derby on 1st July 1978, being a treble at Chepstow and a winner at Newcastle. He had a four-timer on 21st July 1969, being a double at Folkestone and singles at Leicester and Windsor. In all he has had 14 trebles including three in 1978. He has had 79 doubles, of which six have been at Ayr (but none of them in 1978). As expected with such a wide use of different courses, the crossed doubles are very varied, although they often involve local courses such as Brighton and Goodwood.

FIRST WINNER TRAINED

Tamino, Newmarket, Palace House Stakes (now Group 3) £874. Owned by the Duke of Norfolk, ridden by Ron Hutchinson. The race is now more than ten-fold in value—£9,384 in 1978.

HORSES

The number of horses which have won in one season only tends to be proportionately higher than with most trainers but he has shown he can keep a horse in form for years: Daniel, a winner from 1967 to '75,

52

Belper (one-eyed) began winning in 1972 and continued for four more seasons, Traquair won in 1971, '72, '73, '74, '76, '77 and was in the frame eight times in '78. Koala won in five seasons from 1966, Spark in four seasons from 1969 and Kerry Blue in six seasons from 1969. Dunlop trained 80 winners in 1974.

TWO-YEAR-OLDS
There is no particular pattern in his first winning two-year-olds. At one time he introduced early two-year-olds in March. Now mid-May is more usual and occasionally much later. He used to introduce them always at Grade I or II meetings. In the last five years he has opened his two-year-old account at Pontefract, Folkestone, Windsor, Leicester and Lingfield respectively.

PLACED HORSES
Notable 1978 placings include :
Balmerino, second in the Coronation Cup at Epsom, third in the Hardwicke Stakes at Royal Ascot, and second in the Joe Coral Eclipse at Sandown.
Billion, second in the Doncaster Cup.

Mick Easterby

of Sheriff Hutton

Michael Easterby was born in 1931, son of William Easterby, a Yorkshire farmer, point-to-point and amateur N.H. rider in the 1920s. William had several brothers including Walter, who went to Ireland as a whip to a pack of foxhounds, and returned to train successfully in his native county.

Michael's childhood memories are happy ones, but when I talked to him one night in the lounge of the Rutland Arms Hotel, Newmarket, the picture he painted of his early days was one of austerity and struggle.

His father farmed at Thornton Bridge, near Boroughbridge. He then moved to Carr Farm, Fordingham, near Driffield. Next he was at Knayton, near Thirsk and thence to Great Habton. The family moved themselves, their goods and stock by horse and cart in two or three days.

'It was very difficult to make a living and Father kept on going broke in the 1930s. As you know times were hard then. When my uncle Walter came back from Ireland his first job was for Lady Lindsay, and father used to ride for him,' Michael told me. The Countess of Lindsay was a member of the West Riding colliery-owning Shaw family. She and her husband were hunting and N.H. racing enthusiasts. They were supporters of the Middleton and Sinnington Hounds in Yorkshire before moving to Kilconquhar, in Fifeshire, where they hunted and trained jumpers.

John Fairfax-Blakeborough, perhaps the most prolific Turf historian of all time, wrote: 'The Countess is a strong character who knows her own mind, gives very definite orders and expects

54

to have them carried out.' Her colours were white, Lindsay tartan belt, black cap, and it was in these that William Easterby won two races for Lady Lindsay on Amorite at Perth and Wetherby in the autumn of 1926.

'I used to deal in hunters quite a bit as a young man when I worked for my father at home. I suppose I really started out as a dealer and was a nagsman and rough rider,' Michael remembered. 'I started out penniless. The first saddle and bridle I had I borrowed. In fact I used to go hunting bareback because I couldn't afford a saddle.

'The first horse I ever sold was to the Master of the Sinnington, Lord Feversham. He carried him for nine seasons. When I sold him I thought I had got the world—for £70!

'I did two years with Uncle Walter in his racing stable, and then I started out on my own at Sheriff Hutton where I rented a small farm in 1955. By 1957 I hadn't got a penny. I was completely broke. Then I got married. That was it! Alice was a farmer's daughter from nearby Stillington. I am happy to say she saved me and made me.'

Then Mick had some words to say: 'I'll guarantee that behind every good man there is a good wife. I don't know how a man can sail without a good wife. He can sail on his own, but he cannot sail with a bad wife. You can quote that. I'm certain of it. A good wife makes a man better, but if he has a bad wife he is not worth two bob.

'As soon as we got married and worked together I never looked back. Now we farm almost a thousand acres at Sheriff Hutton. We kept adding to our original property by buying farms round about. They are mostly arable.'

He took out a licence to train in 1961. By 1963 he had a small stable of which twelve horses won twenty-two races. He was well on his way.

I asked Michael who gave him the most help before he had the good luck to marry Alice? I suggested perhaps his Uncle Walter, but he brushed this aside unequivocally with, 'Father and Uncle Walter taught me the best way to learn is to teach yourself. Learn from your own mistakes. That's the only way in my opinion.

William Easterby on Amorite, held by his owner, the Countess of Lindsay, in 1926.

But I tell you someone who did help me in a very big way and that was Captain Charles Elsey who trained at Highfields, near Malton, where his son Bill is now. Captain Elsey used to let me take horses on to his gallops occasionally. All I had to start with was a three-furlong plough gallop. I had a bit of grass but it was next to nothing. So I used to run my horses plenty to keep them fit.'

Michael's first winner was Great Rock, owned by Mrs A. C. Straker. The horse, ridden by Jimmy Etherington, won the mile and a half Edinburgh Spring Handicap by a neck from Abbotsbury Abbot. 'It was a tremendous occasion for me but I hardly saw it I was so excited. There were tears in my eyes, and I thought my heart was going to stop beating,' recalled Michael. That nostalgic day was Monday, 17th April 1961. 'Great Rock was a bit of an old dog. I got him fit by riding him out hunting.'

Edward Hide was just about the first jockey consistently to ride

56

winners for Mick, as he is usually called in the racing world. 'He is a very good jockey. Very, very brainy,' he enthused. 'I know Hide better than anyone. He reads the form book very cleverly. He is a fine rider. He never gives a horse too hard a race. A very good thing that. Perhaps he is not the strongest of men in the saddle, but when he has ridden a horse in a race he always comes back and eats up—the horse, that is, not Eddie. I'll tell you another thing. There are few jockeys riding today who know the value of money better than Eddie.

'Jimmy Etherington has ridden for me quite a bit. I've employed Johnny Seagrave and Lionel Brown. I've had them all! I like to use the best jockey I can get and I have never had a stable jockey until now. I've taken on Colin Moss.'

Up to the end of the 1977 flat race season Mick had employed seventy-eight different jockeys to win races for him since he took out a licence to train on the flat in 1961.

Mick was quite definite about the type of horse he favours. 'It's got to be a fairly hard sort of bay horse, well made and well balanced. I know they gallop in all shapes but I must have a well made horse.' He hit this point very hard and repeatedly. 'He must be a good square horse and a good mover. I can't bear to look at him in his box otherwise. I know bad movers gallop fast and so do bad legged horses but I simply must have a good made horse.'

Next came Mick's views on buying horses. They were expressed in his typical, terse and forthright Yorkshire fashion. 'I don't believe in paying big prices,' he said, 'I like to be out of fashion. If you buy in fashion you pay through the nose. The majority of folk at the sales are like sheep. The thing is that when they go one way I go the other.'

'My stable has had wonderful owners for some years. I buy all Mrs Brotherton's horses for her now. She is the best type of owner and I have been lucky enough to saddle something like thirty winners for her in eight years. I suppose the most important of these has been Workboy. Workboy was the only horse she bought herself. He cost about six hundred pounds and I sold him for fifty thousand. Sheriff Hutton was useful and Sweet Nightingale won the Singleton Handicap at Goodwood. She was turned down by two vets and a trainer before I bought her for around a thousand. She was never lame in her life.'

According to Mick, Mrs Brotherton, whose Freebooter won the Grand National in 1950, is a very good loser. Mick can make a mistake with one of her horses and she is 'very nice about it'. She accepts what Mick tells her and 'that's an end of it'.

Mr Charlie Buckton, a farmer, has been a patron of the stable for many years. His best horse to date has been Dutch Gold. Mick bought her dam, My Old Dutch, for two hundred pounds. Dutch Gold won twelve races and her half sister Dutch May won seven.

Mr Len Marginson, a professional backer, is another long-standing patron. He owned Brissenden, a successful two-year-old by Matador. He was unplaced in only one of his ten races and won three. He cost only 1,100 guineas as a yearling and was sold to Venezuela where he did extremely well. 'I bought Len another useful horse—a big 'un called Mighty Faustus—at Newmarket for not much over a thousand,' went on Mick. 'He was by Tamerlane. Everyone said he was too big to race but I knew he would. He was quite a useful two-year-old.

'I have bought Billy Wilson some good winners including Goldwyn for fifteen hundred guineas at Doncaster Sales. She won seven races in a row.'

Mrs Anne Mears, Yorkshire landowner and farmer, is another of Mick's lucky owners. He sold her Polly Peachum for £450 after 'most of a day's friendly haggling' according to Mick.

Mrs Mears, whose Well Packed won the Grand Annual Challenge Cup at Cheltenham in 1966, scored a double at Doncaster on 24th May 1975, with her only two horses in training—Polly Peachum and Scattered Scarlet.

One of Mick's success features is that he is a clever and lucky bargain hunter. I asked him how much he was influenced by pedigree when buying a horse. His answer was, 'A little bit. If I am looking for a filly to breed from, then I do look carefully at the pedigree but otherwise, no. Conformation is nearly everything in my view. A yearling must have balance. I know I keep saying this, but I feel strongly about it. I could draw you what I like but I find it difficult to tell you in words.' Then Mick tried to do just that, and in my opinion hit the target. 'They must,' he said, 'have

The Easterby brothers, Peter (left) and Mick at Newmarket Sales.
(Sport & General)

a good outlook, a good eye and a good ear. Good limbs and good feet. Everything must balance. In addition a horse must have an honest look about him. If you want a good looking horse with a top class pedigree then you can't buy him—he'll cost a fortune which we haven't got.'

Mick has shown the racing world that his ideas and methods of buying and breeding and training horses are thoroughly sound and successful. The fact that in 1976 he won his patrons £111,780, a record for Northern racing, is sufficient proof.

The majority of his big wins have been in sprint races, although he has won the Cesarewitch. That was in 1967 with Boismoss, his first big race winner, bought at Doncaster for a thousand guineas and passed on to Mr John Spriggs. I asked Mick if he had a good bet on Boismoss. His answer will surprise many people who have the impression that he is a 'big' betting trainer. 'No, I didn't,' he said. 'I don't bet much. I had a fiver each way at 66 to 1, if I remember rightly. I don't mind telling you I am a real coward when it comes to betting.' Mick then recalled how he thought Moetchandon which he trained was absolutely sure to win at Newcastle. He decided to have £400 on. He got the money in cash and put the notes in various pockets which he fixed with safety pins. He spent the night on Tyneside and couldn't help thinking about his intended bet. The more he thought about it the more he sweated. He remembered that the sire and dam of Moetchandon did not like soft ground and that's just what the going promised to be for the all important race. So he decided to 'invest' only £200. When he got to the races he heard there was another much fancied runner. He cut his bet to £100, then to £50. Eventually he put on £5. 'Moetchandon won, pulling up!' grinned Mick. There must be many like Mick when it comes to betting. This could be the reason why many of us swim, or just flounder, but do not sink, in racing's difficult seas.

Mick was obviously keen to talk about his high class sprinter Lochnager. Incidentally this horse is named after a mountain in Scotland. Owing to an error the horse's name was registered incorrectly. The final syllable should have been 'ar' and not 'er'. Some TV and sound radio commentators pronounced the horse's

60

*Lochnager (E. Hide) winning the William Hill Sprint Champion-
ship at York.*

name wrongly. This led to a letter or two in the sporting press
from correspondents who like to leap into print. Mick couldn't
have cared less what people called the horse. Lochnager was the
apple of his eye.

Lochnager was by Dumbarnie, out of Miss Barbara, by Le
Dieu d'Or. He won nine races worth £67,765. His chief successes
were the King's Stand Stakes, The July Cup and the William Hill
Sprint Championship.

Now let Mick have his head. This is exactly what he said
between sips of coffee after dinner at the Rutland Arms Hotel:

61

'He was a brilliant horse. Brilliant! He was out of a mare called Miss Barbara. I gave two hundred guineas for her at Doncaster. She was a useful race mare and won six races. So I said, "I'll train every one out of her". She had a winner or two and a few offspring with troubles and then along came Lochnager, bred like the rest of them by Mr Alan Dandy, a friend.'

Mick, after looking at the yearling Lochnager on several occasions, bought him for six hundred guineas. It might be asked why Mr Dandy let the horse go so cheaply. The truth is that he liked him but not well enough to deny Mick taking him on at a reasonable price.

'I offered Lochnager to David Spence who was going down to Newmarket to buy some foals. I showed him the horse. I said, "You won't do better than this. I'll take a thousand for him. Just today you can have him for that". As each day went by at the Sales I upped the price two hundred pounds. The last day came and I offered him at eighteen hundred pounds. Eventually I agreed to toss him whether it was sixteen hundred or eighteen hundred and I won. This was at three o'clock in the morning and I can tell you by then we'd had a few!

'Lochnager was the best horse in the world to train. Marvellous. I didn't train him very hard as a two-year-old because he was very big. He won one £700 race at Ripon with Lionel Brown in the saddle. After that I let him be, and kept him very quiet all winter. I suppose he would have won the King's Stand Stakes as a three-year-old, but he was so well handicapped we just went for the handicaps and won them all.

'He was beaten by Roman Warrior and Import in the Burmah Castrol Ayr Gold Cup. It was a complete mystery to me at the time but now I have thought about it I may have overtrained him. We went from there to Ascot where he won the Bovis Handicap. Then he never looked back.'

The romance and luck of breeding and racing is underlined by the fact that Lochnager the 600 guineas yearling was syndicated as a stallion for £260,000.

I like the handsome tribute paid to Lochnager in the 1967 volume of Timeform Publications' *Racehorses of 1976*, one of the greatest annual productions of Turf literature of all time. In fact I would say it is the greatest. In this the writer says, 'Lochnager swept the board in England's top races for sprinters, achieving a notable treble last achieved in 1949 by Abernant, the only other horse in the post-war era to have won the King's Stand Stakes, the July Cup and the Nunthorpe Stakes in the same season . . . a clean sweep of England's top weight-for-age sprints certainly was exceptional.'

'Lochnager is now at stud at my brother's place at Easthorpe Hall, Malton, Yorkshire. He is easily the best horse I have ever had. Hide and I have often discussed him. We have never seen a horse like him—ever. He could sit with other horses in a race and then you could ask him to accelerate. In a matter of fifty strides he would go two lengths clear of his field and this in a sprint against top horses. I've never seen a horse accelerate like him. It was unbelievable. Honestly, I don't know where his speed came from. I expect you saw him win the July Cup. He produced his fantastic speed there. I didn't know how good he was. Nobody did. The only trouble with him was that when he hit the front he used to pull up.

'He had a super temperament. You could sleep in his box and he wouldn't mind. He was so docile.

'I had to put down an all-weather gallop down specially to train him. That cost me £20,000. It was worth it. Hide said that Lochnager was the best sprinter he had ever ridden.'

Next came the story of Mrs McArdy, Mick's One Thousand Guineas winner in 1977. He explained, 'Lord Grimthorpe bred her. She is by Tribal Chief out of Hanina, by Darling Boy. His Lordship's breeding activities were costing him too much and so he sold me all his horses, every one, including old and barren mares. It was just to get good homes for them really. I think there were eleven of them, and I managed to sell them all in twenty-four hours; but I kept one back, and you can guess which that was.

'When I went home having done this deal with Lord Grimthorpe, I said to my wife, "What on earth am I going to do with them? I may have to give them away. I've got to do something with them otherwise they will be put down, but I have bought one plum. I think she is a fantastic filly and I wonder who I can sell her to?"

My wife said, "Don't forget Mr Kettlewell who gave you an order to buy one six months ago". Then it came back to me. "Of course he did," I said. So I rang him up and told him that I had bought a filly for him and I charged him a thousand pounds. That was Mrs McArdy. I told Bill Kettlewell that she would win the Guineas. My brother Peter can never understand why I entered her in that classic. It is a mystery to him.'

I chipped in here. 'You must have felt in your bones that she had a fair chance of making the grade.'

'Yes, I did,' replied Mick. 'Don't forget she was a yearling and a marvellous individual. To my eye she was absolutely outstanding. You couldn't just paint one better. There was a classic look about her. So I took a chance and put her in the Guineas. I really thought she had got something when she was a yearling. Well, I was even more certain about that when she was a young two-year-old. She was brilliant at home, but when she ran she had three or four races before she won. I couldn't understand it so I got the owner down and said, "Just come and see the filly work. I think she is the best two-year-old I've ever trained". She really worked like a good 'un.

'Then I found something out. She was very shy with other horses. Once she got the message that they were not going to eat her there was no problem. She went to Newcastle, had a bad draw, but away she went and trotted up, hard held by apprentice Neil Crowther. She never looked back. She won the Southern Free Handicap and Tudor Jig won the Northern Free Handicap— quite a double. Incidentally Tudor Jig is a very good horse but he must have heavy ground to give his best. He might have won the Two Thousand Guineas if it had been really soft.

'Well, Mrs McArdy won the One Thousand Guineas and then she ran in the Oaks but not too well. Many people thought the trip of a mile and a half was too far for her but that was not the trouble hat day. She had the virus after the Guineas and she had not

Mrs McArdy (E. Hide) led in by Mrs Kettlewell after winning the 1,000 Guineas at Newmarket. Lord Grimthorpe, her breeder, is just behind (bowler hat). (Sport & General)

properly got over it as events turned out. Mind you I think that a mile and a quarter was about her best trip but she would have been much nearer the winner in the Oaks but for the after-effects of the virus. She recovered her form and won at York. She was not disgraced behind Artaius in Goodwood's Sussex Stakes. She was not really suited by Epsom or Goodwood as a matter of fact because she didn't like coming down hill. She preferred an uphill track. Newmarket suited her very well. It's on the collar. She was sold at the December sales for £154,000 to Bert Firestone and is booked to go to a top stallion in America.

'Lochnager and Mrs McArdy were two very good horses—and you could not have better and nicer people than their owners—the Spencers who own Lochnager, and the Kettlewells who owned Mrs McArdy. Bill Kettlewell has a motel at Aysgarth, near Leyburn, and Mrs McArdy ran in Edith Kettlewell's name.'

Another horse of which Mick has always been fond is Tudor Jig. He was sent down to the sales but there was no bid for him. He belonged to Sir Edwin McAlpine. Mick said to Sir Edwin, 'How much do you want for him?' He replied 'Three thousand guineas.' Mick told Sir Edwin that he liked the horse and that he thought he could sell him. So Mick took him home and asked Mrs Brotherton to buy him, but she wouldn't have him. She didn't like him because he turned his feet out badly. Mick knew that he was a very loose-limbed horse and that he must gallop, judging by the way he moved. Nobody bought him so Sir Edwin kept him. He won the Northern Free Handicap.

Another of Mick's sprinters to carry all before him in the late summer and autumn of 1977 was Jon George. He cost 4,800 guineas at Doncaster as a yearling. He won one race as a juvenile. This was the October Maiden Stakes (5 f) at Doncaster. His price was 20 to 1. Then Mick put him away to give him every opportunity to grow into a strong and keen three-year-old.

'In his early races we asked him to make the running until we found out that he had to be held right up. He began the season (1977) with 7 st on his back, and finished it by proving himself a great handicapper. He won the Vaux Breweries Commemoration of the Royal Jubilee Sprint (5 f), the Tote Sprint Trophy (5 f), the William Hill Portland Handicap (5 f 140 yd), the Burmah Castrol Ayr Gold Cup (6 f) and the Highflyer Stakes (6 f) which were worth £27,863.30p. He was also placed five times in his 17 races in 1977.

'I think he is an intriguing horse to train. To begin with he is very lazy. He refuses to gallop at home and just canters about with a girl on his back, at a pace to suit himself, not her! Anything can beat him on the home gallops, even a bad selling plater. He is looked after at a neighbouring farm where one of my farm men feeds him, and thinks the world of him. But no matter how slow he is at home he is an outstanding performer on a racecourse. As you know he is a very difficult ride. His jockey has to push, push

The finish of the Tote Sprint Trophy at Ascot. Jon George (Willie Carson) wins from Lady Constance and Dancing Circus (Sport & General)

and push. Eventually he gets going, finishes well and doesn't know when he is beat.'

He had seventeen races in 1977. Because he was so lazy at home they had to run him three or four times before he was really fit. He ran in the name of Mrs Newsome. Her husband George was far from well and could not go racing. In fact Mr Newsome asked Mick to run the horse as often as possible in televised races so that he could see him. George Newsome said, prophetically, to Mick, 'I expect I'll be dead by 1978 so get on with the horse now so that we can enjoy having him.' I am happy to say that Jon George responded well to this plan and Mr Newsome saw his victories before he died.

Like the majority of trainers in the North, Mick started with just a handful of horses in 1961. 'I think I had ten, and about a dozen boxes. I have built on to my place as the years have gone by, but I have finished that sort of thing now—definitely, and train between fifty and sixty horses. I've got a first rate head lad, Tom Lynch. He came to me from Charlie Hall, who trained at Tadcaster, and has been with me for fourteen years.'

Mick's chief assistant is Alice, his wife. 'She is a real partner. She is extremely interested in the business and does all the office work,' Mick told me. 'As a matter of fact I spend next to no time in the office, and have very little idea what goes on in there. I hardly ever see an account. My wife does all that for me. I suppose you can say there are two of me. My wife in the office and myself out of it.'

Mick and Alice have two girls and a boy, David, born early in 1977. 'One of my girls, Cherry, is eighteen. The other, Susan, is sixteen, and is still at school. They both love riding. I know Cherry would love to ride in a race, but she is just a little over-weight.

'Like my wife, Cherry is a great help to me and she knows her job as a farmer-trainer's daughter. She can turn her hand to anything. She can work the hay baler, she stacks the straw and drives the combine harvester. She rides out two horses for me every day, she has her own horse and goes eventing with him, and trains a point-to-pointer in her spare time!'

An Easterby family group in the yard at New House Farm.
Alice (left), daughter Cherry, and Mick holding David.

Mick rides out regularly. For ten years as a young trainer he
was hardly off a horse's back. He worked most of the hours in
each day, seven days a week. He says he never had an illness or a
cold for ten consecutive years. His relaxation, at one time very
much part of his business, was fox hunting, and he still does quite
a bit of that. He recalls his many happy days with the Middleton
Hunt when Lord Halifax was Master. He refers to this hunt as
having 'Some of the best country in the land'.

Mick and his head man Tom Lynch break in the yearlings. They
work hard at that. The trainer's only comment in this respect was
'I believe in driving them in strings—and plenty of it.' Like the
majority of trainers I have talked to, he claims that he is easy on
his horses rather than hard when working them. 'I don't hurry my
horses. As you will see from my records they don't really strike
top form till May, after which with a bit of luck we keep winning

Mick's Cesarewitch winner Boismoss leading the string back through the village.

races till the end of September.' That does not mean to say that the flow of winners ceases before the end of the season, for he once had a treble in November. 'I don't hurry them because you have got to remember it's colder up here than in the south. We think that the southern trainers are three weeks in front of us to start with, and can keep their horse going three weeks longer than us in the North at the backend, when our horses' coats start to go. There is no question about it, the southern trainer has a six weeks' advantage on us.'

Just as he likes to remember 1977 as a vintage year, so he would rather forget 1978. It was one of those seasons when little went right. Sickness and its debilitating after-effects devastated most of this trainer's hopes and plans for his horses. This comes to all trainers sooner or later. Dick Hern had three years of the virus in his stable. He got up from the floor to fight back. That's what Mick will do, although he would argue that bad as 1978 was, he was definitely not 'on the floor'.

STATISTICAL RECORDS

Mick Easterby has had 18 seasons as a trainer to date. He has had 472 winners on the Flat, value £506,875 to the end of 1978 and 62 wins under N.H. Rules to end of 1976–7 season.

BIG RACES
The races worth £4,000 or more to the winner (and including Royal Ascot wins) were:

1967

CESAREWITCH	Newmarket	Boismoss	£4,928

1973

GLOBTIK CUP	Goodwood	Dutch Gold	5,624
BOVIS	Ascot	Dutch Gold	4,043

1975

FINCH DECANTER	Ascot	Lochnager	4,146
SEATON DELAVAL	Newcastle	Sweet Nightingale	5,368
BOVIS	Ascot	Lochnager	4,258

1976

TEMPLE	Sandown	Lochnager	6,000
KING'S STAND	Royal Ascot	Lochnager	16,424
GOSFORTH PARK CUP	Newcastle	Lazenby	4,090
JULY CUP	Newcastle	Lochnager	12,258
WM HILL SPRINT (ex Nunthorpe)	York	Lochnager	18,660

1977

TOTE SPRINT	Doncaster	Tudor Jig	4,740
TOTE FREE HANDICAP	Newmarket	Mrs McArdy	6,531
ONE THOUSAND GUINEAS	Newmarket	Mrs McArdy	37,238

VAUX BREWERIES SILVER JUBILEE	Redcar	Jon George	£4,084
TOTE SPRINT TROPHY	Ascot	Jon George	4,588
WM HILL PORTLAND	Doncaster	Jon George	4,714
BURMAH CASTROL AYR GOLD CUP	Ayr	Jon George	12,143
1978			
GOSFORTH PARK CUP	Newcastle	Whenby	9,806

BEST RACECOURSES

Newcastle	46	wins
Ripon	44	,,
Teesside	43	,,
Redcar	38	,,
Thirsk	29	,,
Beverley	28	,,
Doncaster	27	,,
Edinburgh	27	,,
Ayr	26	,,
Catterick	26	,,

JOCKEYS

Eddie Hide	111	wins
Lionel Brown	54	,,
Jimmy Etherington	43	,,
Johnny Seagrave	39	,,
Mark Birch	15	,,
Colin Moss	11	,,

He has employed 78 different jockeys to win races for him on the Flat. Colin Moss, who rode his first winner for him in 1974, rode for him as chief jockey in 1978. Eddie Hide has ridden winners for him ever since he began training. Johnny Seagrave had his first Easterby winner in 1965.

BEST MONTHS

May	95	wins
June	89	,,
August	89	,,
July	80	,,

MULTIPLE WINS

He has had 46 doubles and seven trebles. Four doubles at each of: Thirsk, Teesside, Ripon and Newcastle.

OWNERS

He has had 104 owners up to the end of '77 season, which include himself and his wife. More owners last longer, through more seasons, but with fewer wins (and horses) per season than the other leading trainers. His most successful owner is Mrs Lurline Brotherton with 31 winners since 1970. Others include C. F. Buckton (20 wins), L. Marginson (19), C. F. Spence (16), Mrs Anne Mears (16), John W. Henderson (17) and T. M. Wilson (16).

HORSES

He has had three horses win races over a five-season span: High Table (1965–9) 9 races. Dutch Gold (1971–5) 12 races, Red Rodney (1971–5) 10 races. Fleece, Pal's Passage and Polly Peachum won over four seasons. Ninety-one horses have won races worth £1,000 or more to their owners.

TOP SEASONS

Flat: 1975, 65 races won; 1976, £111,780; 1977, £111,465 prize money.
Jumping: 1974–5, 18 races won; 1975–6, £14,465 prize money.

Dick Hern

of West Ilsley

Not long after William Richard Hern was born at Holford, Somerset, on 20th January 1921, the Hern family went to live at Wick, about eight miles from Bridgwater in the West Somerset Vale. His father, Roy, was a good horseman who loved horses and hunting. Not surprising, therefore, that Dick's earliest recollections are of this happy, carefree life with his parents and his two brothers, Rupert and Michael.

He told me, 'I cannot remember being unable to ride. I think my father probably sat me on a pony before I could walk. He was the greatest influence on the course of my life. He instilled into me his own passionate love for horses.'

Captain Roy Hern farmed about two hundred acres of grass which he kept for his own amusement. The stock consisted chiefly of horses, most of which were hunters, and ponies for the boys. In the Christmas holidays they used to hunt four days a week. On Monday they were out with the Quantock Staghounds. Tuesday, with the West Somerset Foxhounds. Then back with the Staghounds on Thursday, and the Foxhounds on Friday.

Dick told me, 'That was a wonderful part of the world in which to live if you were keen on hunting. Not only could you go out in the autumn and winter, but also in the spring and summer when there was stag hunting. We used to go up into the Quantock Hills which we adored. I have marvellous memories of that very sporting part of England. We got plenty of shooting there too.'

Dick, the eldest of the boys, was sent to preparatory school at Norfolk House, near Beaconsfield. From there he went to Mon-

74

mouth School, followed by a year under the famous Somerset cricketer R. J. O. ('Jack') Meyer, at Millfield.

Dick wanted to go into the Indian Cavalry. When war broke out he was actually at Millfield cramming for the Sandhurst exam, which was cancelled. So Dick and a friend, Peter Dalton-White, borrowed Jack Meyer's car, drove to Bristol and joined up at a reception unit.

'They said we were O.K. because we had School Certificate, and Certificate A which was a school Officers' Training Corps proficiency certificate,' Dick explained. 'Of course we thought we would be going off the next week, but they told us that we would be on the reserve. They didn't really want us till we were nineteen.'

Roy Hern had joined the North Somerset Yeomanry in 1939 and went with the 1st Cavalry Division to the Middle East. When he was invalided home from Palestine he was on the Empress of Britain when she was sunk. He bobbed up all right and later got a job with the Claims Department in the North of Ireland.

So when Dick, aged 18, returned home from Bristol in September 1939 he ran the farm while his father was away. Needless to say that while waiting for his call-up he had some good hunting—at least two days a week. Eventually he was sent to the 55th Training Regiment at Farnborough. He was gazetted to the North Irish Horse and joined them at Westbury on Salisbury Plain. They went in February 1943 to join the First Army in Algiers and were in that campaign right up to the fall of Tunis. The regiment stayed at Bone and in due course went to Naples and fought in the rest of the Italian campaign. This was followed by service in Austria and Germany, and then home.

'Were you thinking about racing in those last months of your service?' I asked Dick.

'Yes, I most certainly was,' he replied. 'I'd ridden in a few point-to-points before the war and I was tremendously keen on racing. Tony Llewellen-Palmer, who commanded the regiment, was another racing enthusiast. We took over some horses from the K.D.G.s and south of the Po we acquired a lot more left behind by the Germans. Michael Pope and I had great fun training a little string on the beach at Rimini. We also raced them on a course made out of the old Ravenna trotting track, but first of all we had to clear the mines. We got the German prisoners out of the cage to do that. We filled in the shell holes and harrowed the ground. It was in fact quite a passable dirt track, four furlongs round. The stands were already there. We ran a tote. I rode a few winners there myself.'

When Dick returned home he did not know quite what to do. Eventually he decided to go to Porlock for a riding instructor's course with Tony Collings. He knew in his heart that whatever he was going to do for a living it had to be with horses. Therefore he felt he ought to seek some qualification. What better than an instructor's certificate? He qualified and Tony Collings asked him to stay on. This Dick did for five years.

In 1952 Michael Pope's assistant trainer, his brother Barry, wanted to go off farming so Michael asked Dick if he would come up from Porlock and help him train at Streatley. They had been, as we have already learned, friends and brother officers during the war so in the circumstances the move was a 'natural'. Dick realised this was a great opportunity, accepted the invitation and stayed with Michael for five years.

Michael had a stable of jumpers and flat-race horses. The experience there was a priceless help to Dick. He did everything there was to do: Mucking out boxes was no problem because as a child he had to look after his ponies. He was also in charge of breaking in the young horses. He wanted to find out about horses in training and to learn the various facets of a trainer's work. The stable routine, how to make entries and forfeits and how to use the Racing Calendar were subjects all new to him. 'Looking back on it all I am reminded that I wanted to train jumpers at that time,' he told me.

'Towards the end of my time at Streatley, Sheilah and I were married. I had known her since the Porlock days. She came on a course there and stayed on to do secretarial work. Her maiden name was Davis. Most of her family were tea planters and she was born in Assam. Her grandparents, the Tweedies, who lived at Petersfield, really brought her up because she was sent to England when quite young.

'During the war Sheilah was a WASBI and was a truck driver

Dick Hern with jockeys Joe Mercer (centre) and Bobby Elliot after riding work.

Dick and Sheilah Hern arrive at the Savoy Hotel for the dinner given when Brigadier Gerard was Champion Racehorse of the Year. (Desmond O'Neill)

in Burma when she was seventeen. Now, as always, she is a tremendous help to me behind the scenes. Like the majority of trainers' wives she helps me entertain owners at home or on the racecourse. Here we have many cottages belonging to the establishment and where the married lads live. This property has to be looked after. You know, decorating, repairs and alterations. Sheilah is responsible for all this. She runs the hostel for single men. She looks after me . . .! And she drives me to and from the races.'

At this point Dick developed a theme which serves to illustrate a facet of a busy trainer's life. He pointed out that with the tremendous amount of office work there is to do it is a waste of time for a trainer to drive himself to the races. 'This applies to me particularly,' he said, 'because I can read in the car. So I do a lot of my work, entries, forfeits and so on while I am being driven there and back.'

78

The other important feature in Dick's working life is that he can sleep when travelling. It does not matter if he is in a plane, train or car, he can sleep if he wants to. This helps him because he usually gets up about a quarter to six. What with going out with the First Lot, then popping into the office, having some breakfast and off to a distant race meeting, he may not be home until seven or eight o'clock at night. He simply has to get his head down sometime and switch off.

Dick stayed in the Streatley job from 1952 to 1957, during which time Michael Pope had some useful but no high class horses. He won good races with Blazon and Luxury Hotel. Both were pretty smart. 'He also had a chaser called Sir John IV on which I was lucky enough to ride a couple of winners,' Dick recalled.

Dick had to wait many years for his first chance to go solo as a trainer. It speaks very well for him that he did not fail, because the new job to which he applied himself was notoriously exacting. It was that of private trainer to the late Major Lionel Holliday, an owner who invested millions of pounds in his racing and breeding and who was always very much the boss. Not only did he not suffer fools gladly but he could be very outspoken and abrupt even to those who wished the old gentleman well and who were not devoid of tact and intelligence. Personally I admired him not only for what he put into horseracing but for his courage. From time to time it was my job to tackle him on behalf of the *Daily Mail* about some aspect of his considerable equine empire. I had to take some stinging rebuffs—quite undeserved, of course! But I must be fair. There were occasions when he was charming, helpful and all was sweetness and light.

I paint this little picture so that what Dick had to say next can be fully understood and savoured : 'In 1957 the late Major Holliday wanted another trainer . . .! I thought, "Well, there's no harm in applying for the job." I had no capital and this was the only way I could see myself setting up as a trainer except on a very small scale.'

So Dick put his head into the lion's mouth. He applied for the job. The old man asked Dick to spend a weekend with him at Copgrove, near Harrogate. 'I went on my own. He did not really want to know about a trainer's wife. Much to my surprise I got the job,' Dick told me. 'I trained for him for five seasons at Lagrange, Newmarket, which at that time was, I think, just about the record for those of us who came after old Bob Colling, who trained for the Major for years.'

The first day Dick rode out with the Holliday string down the road he passed Phantom House where Ryan Jarvis was standing at the gate of his establishment. 'Good morning, Dick,' he greeted Holliday's latest trainer, 'I suppose you have brought your toothbrush. It's all you will need!'

'Amusing though that was, such a remark was not calculated to inspire my confidence,' said Dick. 'But Ryan is a good chap. In fact he is a topper. We have laughed many times since at this welcome to Newmarket.' And Dick and I added a few more chuckles to the tally.

Dick then switched to the good horses he trained for Major Holliday. He spoke of Hethersett, brought down in the Derby, and winner of the St Leger. Dick reminded me, 'I trained Hethersett at the end of my time with Major Holliday. Harry Carr rode the colt. He was an excellent judge and I was jolly lucky to have him ride for me. The first time he was on the colt's back was as a two-year-old in 1961 when they won the Duke of Edinburgh Stakes at Ascot. When he got off him after the race Harry said, "This will be your Derby horse." I have thought many times since of that remark. It revealed an important feature of Harry's skill as a jockey: the colt had given him the right feel. Luckily for me Cecil Boyd-Rochfort hadn't got a Derby horse so Harry rode the colt at Epsom. Hethersett was just where Harry wanted him to be in the race—not far behind the leaders—and in fact he had not even picked him up when Romulus struck into the heels of Crossen and fell. He brought down Hethersett. Harry has got a photograph, taken by a spectator who watched the race on the far side of the course, of Hethersett just going down. Harry is standing up in his irons like a jump jockey landing over Bechers Brook in the National, with his horse's head right on the ground. It is just at that point at Epsom where the horses start to go down hill to Tattenham Corner that the spill took place. It is also there, if you are a spectator on the grandstand, that you lose sight of the runners because of the crowd along the rails on the inside of the course. It is just possible to follow the horses by watching for the jockeys' caps. I was "on" Harry's cap with my binoculars and then suddenly I lost him. A few seconds later the field was round Tattenham Corner and into the straight followed by several loose horses. With that I realised he had gone.'

Breaking into Dick's narrative at this point I remember I had exactly the same experience. I was one of those who hoped

Watched by a gallery of pundits topped by Dick Hern, Hethersett, ridden by Harry Carr, goes to post in his pre-Derby race at Brighton.
(Sport & General)

Hethersett would win the race, and I must admit I was watching him as closely as I could. One moment Harry's cap was there. The next it had disappeared. I realised what had happened at once, but I don't think the television commentators did so because only those who were actually watching the caps of the horses involved in the fall would have suspected disaster. At a difficult phase of the race such as this the race readers would be struggling to identify the leaders. It was not until the field was well into the straight and the riderless horses came into view that thousands, looking and listening in, realised what had happened. The race was won by Mr Raymond Guest's Larkspur (22 to 1), ridden by Neville Sellwood, the top-class Australian jockey who was killed in a riding accident. Incidentally Larkspur was the first of Vincent O'Brien's five Epsom Derby winners up to and including The Minstrel (1977).

Seven horses fell in Larkspur's Derby. The pile up was missed by the ITV cameras because one was not sited to record, without obstruction by the crowd, incidents on this section of the course. The following year and, I believe, in succeeding years, a camera has been placed to cope with an eventuality such as this. As a matter of fact it was not the first time that horses had come to grief at or near that spot.

Hethersett got some nasty cuts. He'd been head over heels so it is not surprising that he broke the tree of his saddle. The fall at that pace going down hill really shook him up. In fact when at exercise he did not go out of a walk for a month after the Derby. That brings us to the beginning of July which just gave Dick time to get him ready to run at Goodwood at the end of the month. When he ran there in the Gordon Stakes he was short of his best and the ground was possibly a bit firm for him. The race was won by Gay Challenger, from Ireland. In Dick's opinion it might have been better to have waited for the Voltigeur, a few weeks later at York. 'Anyway,' he said, 'Harry didn't give him a hard race at Goodwood for the ground had got a bit firm. By the time the Voltigeur came round in mid-August Harry was suffering from the effects of another fall. So Frank Durr rode the colt at York and he beat Miralgo by a short head with Monterrico three lengths back in third place.'

Harry Carr rode Hethersett in the Leger. He started at 100 to 8 and won very easily from his York rivals Monterrico and Miralgo. The ground was just right for him.

'He was a lovely little horse with a marvellous temperament,' Dick enthused. 'After the Derby when he was on the easy list he never got fresh. He used to stand quietly out in the yard when we put the hosepipe on him. He didn't mind the cars coming in and out. He took it all as a matter of course. He was a real gentleman.'

Lionel Holliday had won the Oaks with Neasham Belle in 1951. She was trained by Geoffrey Brooke and ridden by Stan Clayton who is Dick's assistant at West Ilsley. Naturally the Major was very keen to win another classic, particularly the Derby, but he took the Hethersett disappointment remarkably well.

A week before the Derby, Clive Graham, then The Scout of the *Daily Express*, went to Newmarket to try to buy Hethersett for an American. Dick related: 'Clive had the cheque made out for £100,000 which in those days was a real fortune. It was an "easy day" with the string at exercise in the paddock. The horses were walking round and I was sitting on my hack. Clive pulled the cheque out of his pocket and said to me with a chuckle, "Have you ever seen one made out for as much as that?" Needless to say I had not. Anyway the old man wouldn't sell.'

About half an hour after the Derby, when Major Holliday was satisfied that Hethersett was not seriously hurt by his fall he went to his car and set off back to Yorkshire with his chauffeur Breen. The old major never spoke until he got to Doncaster and then he said to Breen, 'We'll win the Leger with that horse.'

Dick's next comment on his patron was that he was a hard man but absolutely straight. If his horses didn't win they always had to do their best to get a place. Even the two-year-olds first time out had to be ridden out.

'I was lucky in that I had some good horses when I was training for him,' said Dick. 'There are the four I had in the yard at one time,' and he indicated a single frame above the fireplace which held pictures of a quartet of racehorses. They were Hethersett, Avon's Pride, Proud Chieftain and Nortia. Avon's Pride won the Cesarewitch, and both Proud Chieftain and Nortia won the Magnet Cup at York which of course vastly pleased their owner.

'I don't think people realise what a good horse Proud Chieftain was, although he was not quite the tops. He died young and would have made a marvellous stallion,' said Dick. Proud Chieftain was a great challenge to Dick and his staff because when the colt was a foal he was badly infected with red worm. This affected his digestion so that as a yearling he was very weak. Dick could not run him as a two-year-old. His droppings were always very loose. It was only when he was three (1960) that his insides began to work properly. He was still weak when he won the Column Produce Stakes and was beaten in the Chester Vase by Mr Higgins. The Roodee ground was too soft for him. He ran very well in the Derby, and was second in the Eclipse to St Paddy.

Major Holliday used to go to Lagrange to see the horses regularly at the Newmarket meetings. He didn't stay with the Herns because he had his own little house in Park Lane in Newmarket. He kept a hack on which he rode out and it was then that he and Dick got on pretty well together. 'Apart from the horses we used to talk about hunting,' Dick recalled. 'He loved it and so do I. He used to tell me stories of when he was Master of Foxhounds, particularly of the Derwent, the Badsworth and the Grove. He had, I think, been a Master of Hounds since before the 1914–18 war.

'We didn't have a row to finish up with, and in many ways I was sorry to go. It was just that when Jack Colling was retiring and Jakie Astor had bought the place here he wanted someone to take over from Jack. I was offered the job and took it.

'I shall always be very grateful to Major Holliday for giving me the chance to train high class horses. When I first went to Lagrange I had two great allies and helpers. They were Jim Meaney, his old head man, who had been with him for years and Stan Clayton who was first jockey to the stable for the first two seasons I was there. He knew Major Holliday backwards. Three years ago Stan came to me here. He is a wonderful chap. He gets

Dick Hern with some of his staff and string at his West Ilsley stables. (Daily Mirror/Syndication International)

on with everybody and is extremely conscientious. No day is too long for him. He has a great sense of humour and keeps a smile on his face.'

When Dick went to West Ilsley it was more or less an all-Astor concern. Jakie and his brother Bill, the late Lord Astor, had big strings there. 'This was the time when Provoke won the 1965 St Leger and we had quite a good run,' said Dick. 'We knew Provoke loved the soft ground and he had run a good race in the Melrose Handicap at the York Ebor Meeting when he beat by a head Sam Hall's Santa Vimy which they thought was "past the post". It was only a handicap but he raced very gamely. I knew there was some improvement in him because he had always been a backward animal. He was plagued with little splints and was rather soft boned. Nearly all the sons and daughters of Aureole stay and improve with age. Provoke was no exception. The Leger was his day.'

Dick, Sheilah, Joe Mercer and his wife, Anne, stayed for the Leger at Punch's hotel on the old A1, south of Doncaster. They played cards the night before the Leger in one of their rooms. They could hear the rain coming down and hitting the window panes. They were loving it because whatever chance Provoke had, the more it rained the better he would go. Doncaster is a very well drained course and it has to have inches of rain to make it soft. It rained and rained. It was still raining at the time of the race.

'The amusing thing was that the More O'Farrells had laid on a party to celebrate the much expected victory of Meadow Court,' said Dick. 'Everything including the champagne was ready for this at Punch's. I will never forget how marvellous they were. When Provoke (28 to 1) beat Meadow Court (11 to 4 on) by ten lengths they had the party and asked Jakie Astor, Sheilah and I to come to it. We could not have been more pleased. I always hope I could have behaved as well if the position had been reversed. But to go back to the race for a moment. There was so much mud on all the colours that when the racecourse commentator saw a horse winning by a street he thought it must be Meadow Court. Most people were shouting Meadow Court home but I knew the horse in front was mine!'

The finish of the 1974 St Leger, won by Lady Beaverbrook's Bustino ridden by Joe Mercer, from Giacometti (Lester Piggott) and Riboson (Jim Lindley). (Sport & General)

Dick acknowledged that it had been great fun training for the Astors. 'We had plenty of luck, good and bad, and of course there was one shocking period of misfortune.'

Provoke's classic triumph in 1965 saved the Hern string from a lean season for it was that year which saw the onset of the equine flu. Dick endured three seasons which almost finished him, at least for the time being, as a trainer at West Ilsley.

'We had an absolutely terrible time,' he said with some feeling. 'The flu completely crucified my string. It was so bad we even took the tan out of the covered ride and replaced it with sand just in

87

case there were any bugs in the tan. That's how desperate we had
become. It was nearly driving me mad but I realised there was
little to be done except sweat it out, and as you will agree, three
years is a mighty long sweat!'

Dick was thankful it went when it did. The horses couldn't go
at all. Also it was not realised that they were still sick animals
when they appeared to have recovered. Dick admits to hindsight
but what he says he should have done was to have stopped them
working as soon as there was the first sign of trouble. 'The form
is to give them plenty of time to get over the flu and then follow
this with a little bit of trotting,' he told me.

'Now one can vaccinate against an equine flu,' said Dick. 'I
would not dream of not doing so, knowing as I do what can happen
if you don't. Let me give you an example. Several years ago I had
a backward two-year-old turned out at a yard not very far from here
where you can rest animals. It is also a sort of transit camp for
horses. My horse went there for a month or so. Shortly after he
got there six show jumpers came in from Hickstead. They
arrived with temperatures of 106 and were coughing their heads
off. Every other animal in that yard coughed within four or five
days except my two-year-old which had been vaccinated. That, to
my mind, was a wonderful test because my animal was at a very
low ebb. He had recently been castrated. If he was going to
catch anything he would have caught it then.'

Both Provoke and Craighouse who won the Irish St Leger in
the same year were infected by the flu in 1966 when they were
four-year-olds. 'Neither of them was worth a carrot—as a racehorse—afterwards,' their trainer reminded me. 'It finished Provoke
and it finished Craighouse too—he was last in the Paradise Stakes
at Ascot. It was the first time the disease was known in England.
Nobody really understood it.'

Both colts were sold to Russia as stallions. When they got to
Moscow there was no ramp to get them off the plane so they
wheeled up a passenger ramp with steps, put some wire netting on
it, straw on top of that and walked them down that. Neither horse
turned a hair. The Russians had bad luck with those horses.
Provoke died quite soon. Craighouse headed the list of winning
stallions but he too died years before he should have done.

*   *   *

When the late Lord Astor died his stud was sold, mostly to America. The horses he had in training were bought by Lord Rotherwick who is one of Dick's patrons. There is still some of that blood at West Ilsley. Jakie Astor has horses with Dick but he sold the training establishment to Sir Michael Sobell when Gordon Richards gave up training.

Lady Beaverbrook, one of Dick's patrons and whose racing manager is Sir Gordon Richards, has spent hundreds of thousands of pounds on bloodstock. Her lucky number is seven and that is the number of letters in each horse's name. The horses which have brought her trainer most credit are probably Bustino, Boldboy and Relkino. Dick said of Bustino: 'He was a grand racehorse, very tough and genuine and he got the trip well. What he wanted was a good pace. I always thought he was unlucky in the 1974 Derby in which he was fourth after a terrible run. Joe Mercer could never get where he wanted. Don't forget that he had twice beaten the winner, Snow Knight, at Sandown and in Lingfield's Ladbroke Derby Trial. He trotted up in the St Leger, comfortably beating Giacometti. As he had previously won the Voltigeur at York he can be said to have had an outstanding season.

'When he ran the next year in the King George and Queen Elizabeth Diamond Stakes and gave Grundy such an exciting and hard race he had not been out since the Coronation Cup at Epsom in May.'

Dick maintains that if he had been able to run the four-year-old in the Princess of Wales's Stakes at Newmarket, which circumstances prevented, then Bustino would have given Grundy an even harder race at Ascot and might have cracked the three-year-old in what has been called 'The Race of the Century' and which is the title of a sound and entertaining book by Christopher Hawkins.

My host then paid a warm tribute to Sir Gordon Richards: 'He is a wonderful man. Twenty-six times champion jockey, his memory goes back a long way. The experience he has had with horses and people is unsurpassed. He knows so much about the ancestry of horses in my yard. He is certain to have ridden one or more of the forbears of each one of them. That is a great help to both of us because that sort of experience and knowledge of family traits goes a long way to enable us to handle and place horses successfully.

'It is also great to be in his company. He comes down here twice a week when the horses work and he rides out on his pony. I am always delighted to have him here.'

Now let's turn to Relkino, whose success, after early setbacks, is a clear example of his trainer's brilliant horsemastership.

Relkino only ran twice as a two-year-old in 1975. He is by Derby winner Relko, out of Pugnacity (one of the late Major Lionel Holliday's breed but not trained by Dick Hern).

The first time Relkino ran he won Newbury's Ecchinswell Stakes (6 f) readily by four lengths from Quite Candid. Dick commented on this race, 'I don't think Joe Mercer could touch one side of him. The colt jumped out of the stalls and he just sat against him. The horse simply strode along and won. The next time he ran, in the Washington Singer Stakes over six furlongs at Newbury in August, he started 2 to 1 on favourite and finished last of five. The race was won by Lady Beaverbrook's other runner, Homeboy, at 14 to 1.

'Well, there was absolutely no doubt that Relkino was below par. His blood count was not right and I suspect there was a mild virus in the yard.'

The outcome of this race would appear to have been embarrassing for Dick, but I quickly point out that Homeboy was not trained by him but by Ian Balding, at Kingsclere.

Dick reminded me that, 'Relkino was thought to be a good thing. Only a matter of going down and coming back but the colt was never going after two furlongs.'

Apart from this setback the problem Dick always had with Relkino was that in his work at home he was perfectly all right as long as he was kept covered up. On the racecourse as soon as the stalls opened he would be off like a rocket. It was impossible to restrain him. Sometimes he was lucky if there was a good gallop and he tracked the right horse.

'He was lucky in the Derby,' said Dick. 'He ran a wonderful race to be second to Empery but he didn't quite last it out.'

It was not until Relkino's four-year-old career that Dick found the solution to the colt's problem, i.e. a bit to suit Relkino's mouth and which enabled his jockey to control him. The colt had been ridden for some months in a Citation bit, in fact he wore one in the Derby and in his early races in 1977. Then in the Sussex Stakes at the main Goodwood meeting, in July, Dick tried the colt in a double-mouthed snaffle. This has single rings at each side of the mouth and has two mouth pieces the joints of which are slightly offset. Thus both joints are not exactly in the middle of a horse's mouth.

When fitted with this Relkino could not, in the words of his trainer, 'lay too hard on it'. Willie Carson then found he could ride him like any ordinary horse and settling him very well in the Sussex Stakes finished third to Artaius and Free State.

'Then we lined him up for the Benson and Hedges Gold Cup at York,' Dick said. 'They went a cracking good gallop. When Willie produced him, having had him beautifully settled, it was just a case of—ping! That was it. Relkino really dominated the field.' He beat Artaius by four lengths.

That case history had a happy ending and demonstrates how a potentially good horse could have been wasted but for a skilful trainer's observation and ability. Relkino, winner also of the £17,033 Lockinge Stakes at Newbury, added another £52,867 to his tally by his York victory. He now stands at Lord Fairhaven's Barton Stud.

Lady Beaverbrook's Boldboy is one of those horses which have genuinely captured the imagination of the racing public. There have been others such as Brown Jack, Arkle, Sugar Palm, The Tetrarch, Mumtaz Mahal, Brigadier Gerard and Red Rum which have made bigger names for themselves, but Boldboy is a proved crowd puller. The bay son of Bold Lad and Solar Echo has plenty of fans who send him presents, letters and cards. Certainly up to the end of 1977, by which time he had won 12 races, age had not wearied him. His form was better than ever. Just when some of his greatest admirers were saying, 'Surely he cannot win with that enormous weight?', up he would come. There he would be in the winner's enclosure and Willie Carson's face would crease into a smile for the umpteenth time. It happened again in 1978 when he won the Ladbroke Abernant Stakes at Newmarket in April, carrying 9 st 12 lb.

Boldboy is in fact one more example of how a good trainer can help a difficult horse to success. Boldboy was a problem as a two-year-old and like Relkino only ran twice at that age. He made his debut in the Erroll Maiden Stakes (5 f) at Ascot in June 1972. This was won by Sandford Lad, probably the best horse trained on the Flat by Ryan Price. Boldboy was fourth of nine.

Dick said of Boldboy : 'He was a terribly difficult two-year-old. The Nasrullah male line is inclined to be temperamental and Boldboy was no exception. He never really accepted starting stalls. Piggott rode him first time out at Ascot. I told Lester to win if he could but on no account to be hard on him otherwise he might be ruined. I asked Lester to try to teach the colt something about racing. When Lester got off him he said to me, "He'll be all right", which was quite a long speech for him!

'Next time we ran him was at Newbury. He was in the last race (Harwell Maiden Stakes, 5 f, 16th September). We had already won that afternoon with Colum and Donello. Boldboy, favourite at 5 to 2, was really the best thing of the day but he would not go in the stalls and was withdrawn.' The race was won by the John Sutcliffe-trained Flyer.

Dick, obviously, had to try to get the colt used to the stalls. The trouble was that he attempted to put all four of his legs through to the stall next door through the gap between the side of the stall and the ground. Dick believes that it was claustrophobia. The next move was to fit a special attachment to the West Ilsley training stall so that the side boards went right down to the ground. Thus there was no gap through which he could thrust his feet but Boldboy would not get used to the stalls.

'I was always afraid that the jockey would get hurt because the colt would throw himself violently about when he went in,' said Dick. 'Of course it was possible to get permission to go into the stalls last, but it was impossible to tell if there would be some other drama. Another horse playing up or backing out. However considerate the starter, there are times when he cannot avoid leaving a horse in the stalls longer than he wants to be there.'

Dick decided that it was no good running him in a maiden when there would be twenty-five or more runners. This would guarantee a difficult starting stalls scene for Boldboy. So the high class Middle Park Stakes was chosen for the colt's next race. The size of the field for this two-year-old 'classic' is usually in single figures and so it was on this occasion. There were seven runners.

'Brian Proctor rode him. He is a grand chap. He rides all the difficult animals, schools horses through the stalls and hardly ever gets a fancied ride because he is put up on the green ones, backward ones and things that want experience, things with very little chance and so on.

'Of course Boldboy was quite up to the Middle Park standard. When I gave Proctor a leg up on him I said, "Now then, Brian! This is your chance to win the Middle Park", and I really meant it. Unfortunately for Brian that sort of thing rarely happens. He did wonderfully well, got him in the stalls, got him off and rode a good race. He looked like winning for a long way and finished fourth of the seven runners, less than four lengths behind the winner, Tudenham, owned by Brook Holliday.

'Before the Middle Park I had to give the colt a tremendous lot of work. You see I had to be hard on him to get on top of him so that he would consent to go into the stalls. In the circumstances he ran a marvellous race.

'Well, we had to make a decision to geld him or not. I would, of necessity, have had to be very hard on him all through that winter to keep him in control for racing as a three-year-old, so regretfully we decided to geld him. He would have been too great a problem for training and racing had he been left an entire horse.'

His best season was 1977, with five victories. By the end of 1978, Boldboy had won 13 races (one in France) from 6 furlongs to one mile. They were worth £89,514.53p. His most valuable wins will be found in the statistics.

So there is the inside story of how one more outstanding racehorse came through trials and tribulation before he galloped so consistently and impressively to numerous victories.

I then asked Dick how he became one of the Queen's trainers. Dick replied, 'Funny thing. I don't think I can remember the first approach. I think it may have been by Richard Shelley, who was then the Queen's Stud Manager. I imagine it must have been him because it was before Lord Porchester became racing manager. 1966 was my first season as one of the Queen's trainers. I began when Cecil Boyd-Rochfort finished. I had only yearlings to start with.

'The Queen generally comes down in the spring to watch work and then maybe again in the summer and possibly in the winter.'

Her Majesty sometimes visits the Old Rectory, the Herns' home,

Joe Mercer tells Her Majesty the Queen and her racing manager Lord Porchester how he won the 1,000 Guineas on Highclere. (Sport & General)

for breakfast or tea because if she comes to see the horses work it is most likely to be First Lot and she may stop and have breakfast afterwards. If her visit is to evening stables then she may have tea with Dick and Sheilah beforehand.

I asked Dick if in 1976 he thought the Queen's Dunfermline would make a classic filly. 'Well, I knew she was one of the best staying two-year-old fillies. After all she ran Miss Pinkie to half-a-length over a mile at Ascot in September. Triple First was third, one and a half lengths behind her. Obviously there were none much better than them.' He realised that Dunfermline would have to improve a little bit if she was to be one of the tops. It was quite on the cards that she would do so because in her races as a two-year-old once or twice she looked like coming to win and then carried her head a little bit high and did not really get down to work. As a result of this some people thought she was not genuine and suggested that she might need blinkers. Joe Mercer always said, 'No! Don't do that. She is only green'. He was right.

'So as I say,' Dick went on, 'it was reasonable to suppose there was improvement in her when she learned more about racing. Well, as a three-year-old she was a different filly. We all saw how well she came to win the Oaks, and in the St Leger she stayed better than Alleged. I'll tell you this—if we had not had a rattling good gallop set by Gregarious at Doncaster we might have been beaten. He went on with Alleged and made absolutely certain of a cracking pace which suited the Queen's filly but not Alleged.'

Dunfermline ran three times in 1978. She reappeared in the Hardwicke Stakes ($1\frac{1}{2}$ m) at Royal Ascot but well though she ran she could not master the French colt Montcontour. She was prominent for a long way in the King George and Queen Elizabeth Diamond Stakes in July but faded in the last quarter mile. Her final race, the Geoffrey Freer Stakes at Newbury, saw her run fourth to Ile de Bourbon. She won £8,041 in place money so although it could be said that her third season was slightly dis-appointing, she paid her way and won about £3,000 more in 1978 than her three-year-old half-sister Tartan Pimpernel which carried the Royal colours to victory in York's Galtres Stakes and was fourth in the Park Hill Stakes.

Undoubtedly the two best animals Dick has trained for Her

Majesty The Queen are Dunfermline and Highclere, winner of the 1974 One Thousand Guineas.

Highclere was not difficult to train in that she would always do her work at home. She was quite highly strung, but she managed to behave herself most of the time.

'There was plenty of fire inside Highclere,' Dick explained. 'A lot of credit must go to Betty Brister who did her. She was not an easy filly to look after and to do. If she had an indifferent groom it might have ruined her. She was a very sound filly with good legs so there were no problems about whether one dared to work her or not. Most of Queen's Hussars' stock are like that. For instance Brigadier Gerard was a very sound horse.

'I felt very proud of Brigadier Gerard,' Dick enthused. 'He was the sort of horse every trainer dreams of having because he seemed to be head and shoulders above his contemporaries. After a time I could never see him getting beaten as long as we kept him well.'

Naturally I responded tactfully, for there is no doubt that 'The Brigadier' was a great and consistent horse, but he was not un-beatable as we saw once, and very nearly thrice!

Dick took this point up at once. 'He was very nearly beaten by the four-year-old Rarity in the Champion Stakes which he won in 1971 and 1972. There was good reason for this because he was not at his best on soft ground and it was just that, when Rarity ran him to a short head in 1971. Rarity was much fancied to beat him because he revelled in the mud. He probably got that quality from his sire Hethersett.'

I remember another day when the conditions were all against Brigadier Gerard and that was at Royal Ascot in 1971 when Mrs John Hislop's great horse was bogged down in very soft ground in the St James's Palace Stakes. The colt, under Joe Mercer's driving, showed tremendous courage to hold off the Lester Piggott-ridden Sparkler by a head. In the following year Brigadier Gerard was again opposed by Sparkler over the same course and distance, in the Queen Elizabeth II Stakes. This time the ground was firm. With the same jockeys as in 1971 'The Brigadier' beat his rival by six lengths and lopped a second off the best recorded time for the dog-legged Old Mile.

Now let's hear what Dick had to say about Brigadier Gerard's three lengths defeat by Roberto, the 1972 Derby winner, in York's Benson and Hedges Gold Cup the same year: 'I always think that the reason he was beaten is possibly that he had run in the King George VI and Queen Elizabeth Diamond Stakes over a mile and a half at Ascot and which he won.

'You could say he didn't stay a mile and a half. Oh yes, I know he won over that distance at Ascot and beat some very good horses but the effort of doing so—of running out of his distance—

A happy Willie Carson brings home the Queen's Dunfermline to a comfortable win in the Oaks from Freeze the Secret (Gianfranco Dettori) and Vaguely Deb (Bruce Raymond). (Sport & General)

just took the edge off him. I don't think that next time out, at York, he probably gave quite his best running, although it must be said that not only did Roberto break the course record but so did our horse.'

After that great drama Brigadier Gerard came back to a mile and won the Queen Elizabeth II Stakes at Ascot and then the one-and-a-quarter mile Champion Stakes at Newmarket, thus again proving himself the magnificent racehorse we knew him to be. Brigadier Gerard won the Middle Park Stakes and three other races as a two-year-old; the Two Thousand Guineas, the St James's Palace Stakes, the Sussex Stakes and the Goodwood Mile as a three-year-old. The following year he won the Lockinge Stakes at Newbury, the Prince of Wales Stakes at Royal Ascot, and the Eclipse Stakes and Westbury Stakes at Sandown. In all he won seventeen of his eighteen races and his total earnings were £253,024 and 70p!

A brief perusal of the statistics at the end of this chapter will show just how all-conquering this colt was and how he really 'cleaned up' big prizes. For those who would wish to read a whole book on this horse there is only one answer: *The Brigadier*, published by Secker and Warburg and charmingly written by his part owner-breeder, John Hislop.

Dick Hollingsworth is an owner-breeder, member of the Jockey Club, who for many years has regularly bred good middle-distance and staying horses from his comparatively small stud. As an observer of the racing scene I have come to expect half-a-dozen winners or more in his colours each season.

Dick Hern has played his part in maintaining this run of success, notably with Sea Anchor and Buoy, the better horse of the two. 'Buoy was a great horse with a superb action. He wasted absolutely no time in the air,' Dick told me. 'You hardly ever get a horse his size—he was at least sixteen-three—with so much quality. He won the Coronation Cup, run over the Derby course at Epsom, and made every yard of the running. I shall always believe he ought to have won the St Leger. To be frank I shall never understand how Peleid beat him, but there you are, that's how the game goes sometimes. Sea Anchor was not quite up to

After winning the King George VI and Queen Elizabeth Diamond Stakes at Ascot on Brigadier Gerard, Joe Mercer chats to Dick Hern. (Sport & General)

Buoy's class but he was a very good resolute stayer. Don't forget that he won the Goodwood Stakes with ten stone and also took the Doncaster Cup.'

I asked Dick what he considered to be the first good horses he trained. Naturally he took me back to his Holliday period by nominating Galivanter, a sprinter, and None Nicer, a top class filly. Galivanter, by Golden Cloud, did not win as a two-year-old but he was always in the frame in his five races which included a one-and-a-half length defeat by Masham in Royal Ascot's New Stakes (1958). He quickly made amends as a three-year-old, winning five of his eight races and being placed in the remainder. He was beaten only half a length by the five-year-old Right Boy in the Nunthorpe, currently known as the William Hill Sprint Championship. None Nicer, by Nearco out of Phase, was one of the three-year-olds Dick took over when he went to Lagrange (1958). He described her as a really tough and good filly. She won the Lingfield Oaks Trial, the Ribblesdale at Royal Ascot, and the Yorkshire Oaks. She was fourth in the Oaks behind François Dupré's Bella Paola, runner up to Guersillus in Goodwood's Gordon Stakes and to Alcide in the St Leger. Dick's comment on that Doncaster classic was, 'She should have won the Park Hill at Doncaster in a canter but the old major wanted to run her in the Leger. She had no chance of beating Alcide but she ran a marvellous race. We kept her, intending to campaign her as a four-year-old, but she didn't stand training.'

Dick's favourite racecourse is Newbury. It is also where he has been most successful, as shown in the statistics. 'There is not much wrong with it,' he said. 'The main snag is the difference the draw can make to the sprint races. We have done well there and I suppose it is one of "our" courses. It involves no travelling which is a bonus to a trainer like me! I can go out with the Second Lot after breakfast, see 'em work, come home, change and have plenty of time to be at Newbury for the first race. Apart from the winners we have had there, that's why I like it so much.'

Dick and Sheilah live in the village of West Ilsley about half a mile from the stables. Their home is a charming and comfortable old rectory, typical of the comparatively large houses in which most clergymen and their wives today are usually only too glad not to live. When I called there in the very early spring there were thousands of snowdrops under the budding lime trees and here and there clumps of orange, white and mauve crocuses. No wonder Dick said of his wife, 'She wouldn't like to move from here. She has done an awful lot in the garden and is very attached to it. We have lived here getting on for fifteen years. We might have to go one day. You never know.'

The trainer's house is really Hodcott, near the stables. Jack Colling lives there and has the right to do so for his life time.

Although the Old Rectory features mostly in local church history the Herns are not the first racing people to live there, for it was once the home of Maitland-Wilson, a Jockey Club Handicapper.

Horses were trained at Hodcott by Frank Barling, father of Geoffrey, trainer of Tower Walk and other outstanding horses. Frank trained at Hodcott before World War I after which he was for a short time at Falmouth House, Newmarket and won the 1919 Derby with Lord Glanely's Grand Parade. Incidentally Richard Onslow reminds us in his fine history of Newmarket, entitled *The Heath and the Turf* (Arthur Barker Ltd) that Lord Glanely in due course sent his horses to be trained at Lagrange (where, as I have related, Dick Hern trained for Major Holliday) and anglicized the stable's name to The Grange. The establishment was built by my great-grandfather, 'Old' Tom Jennings. He called the place Lagrange in honour of Count Lagrange, a son of one of Napoleon's marshals, and owner of Gladiateur, Triple Crown winner in 1865, and Fille de L'Air, the 1864 Oaks heroine. Both were trained by 'Old' Tom. 'Young' Tom, his son, trained at Phantom House from the gates of which Ryan Jarvis so humorously welcomed Dick to Newmarket.

After World War I such men as Captain Gooch and Eric Stedall preceded Jack Colling, who sent out Ambiguity from Hodcott to win the 1953 Oaks for Lord Astor. Joe Mercer rode Ambiguity and scores of other winners trained there. When this exceptionally stylish and talented rider retired from being first jockey at West Ilsley, several owners commissioned Adriana

Zaefferer to paint the heads of the Classic winners Joe had ridden, namely Ambiguity, Provoke, Bustino, Highclere, Sharp Edge (Irish Two Thousand Guineas), Brigadier Gerard and Craighouse (Irish St Leger).

Like the majority of leading flat-racing trainers today Dick believes that he is not severe on his horses. 'I try not to be hard,' he says. 'I like to put myself in the position of the animal. Obviously they can only go on working and racing if they are enjoying it. I have to live with the horses. I see them every day and I like to keep them contented and fit. Training on the downs here is a lovely way of conditioning horses because you have not got to be too hard on them. They are often "on the collar", climbing. Downland gallops are nearly all on the collar. That's why here you can keep animals fresher and sweeter than they do at Newmarket, where of course there are marvellous facilities but you have to be that much harder on horses.'

Sale ring habitués will often see Dick but mostly when he is selling horses from his stables to make room for younger stock. He does buy a few yearlings but to quote him, 'I am pleased to say that most of my owners breed their own. Fillies I have trained go back quite often to their owners' studs. For instance I now have a colt by Mill Reef out of the Queen's mare Highclere. In fact he is her first foal and is called Milford. Well named, don't you think, because, as you know, the Queen's racing manager Lord Porchester lives at Highclere and the name of his home is Milford.'

The Queen's and, incidentally, Dick's first Derby winner? At least it can be said that Milford is bred like one. He showed promise when runner-up to the brilliant Tromos at Ascot in September 1978. Next time out he started favourite in the Newmarket Houghton Stakes (7 f) and was a slightly disappointing second, beaten four lengths by One in a Million, admittedly a filly of potential class.

The finish of the 1974 1,000 Guineas shows Highclere's narrow victory from Polygamy.

*   *   *

Like the skilled operator and workman that he is, Dick kept battling along through 1978 picking up races here and abroad. He did not win a Classic. He had no knockout punch but he kept scoring points and did very well with such horses as Lord Porchester's Smuggler which twice beat Shangamuzo, the Ascot Gold Cup winner—in the Yorkshire Cup and in the Henry II Stakes at Sandown in May; Sir Michael Sobell's filly Cistus, winner of four races including the Group 2 Nassau Stakes at Goodwood and the Prix de L'Opéra worth £16,667 at Longchamp in October; and Lord Rotherwick's Homing, successful five times including wins at Longchamp and Ascot in September.

The Queen's filly Rhyme Royal won four nice handicaps and Lord Porchester's colt Town and Country won five times including the £9,968 John Smith's Magnet Cup.

There can be no doubt that the partnership of Dick Hern and Willie Carson—champion jockey of 1978, thanks in great part to the fine rides provided by Dick—will be among the big winners in 1979 and probably for years to come.

STATISTICAL RECORDS

Dick Hern has had 21 seasons as a trainer and 1,007 winners on the Flat in Britain for a total of £2,051,819 in first prize money. He has won 317 races worth more than £10,000 to the owner between 1957 and 1977 inclusive. He has won a further 42 races worth £2,000 or more to the owner in 1978.

TRAINERS' TABLE

1970	5th	50 winners of	£58,742
1971	3rd	57 winners of	£141,531
1972	1st	42 winners of	£206,767
1973	8th	62 winners of	£90,588
1974	2nd	55 winners of	£201,850
1975	6th	56 winners of	£90,138
1976	5th	69 winners of	£153,298

| 1977 | 2nd | 74 winners of £338,471 |
| 1978 | 4th | 74 winners of £253,815 |

BIG RACES
The races worth £4,000 or more to the winner were:

1958

| RIBBLESDALE | Ascot | None Nicer | £4,370 |
| YORKSHIRE OAKS | York | None Nicer | 6,802 |

1961

| MAGNET CUP | York | Proud Chieftain | 4,211 |

1962

| GREAT VOLTIGEUR | York | Hethersett | 4,200 |
| ST LEGER | Doncaster | Hethersett | 31,407 |

1964

ZETLAND GOLD CUP	Redcar	Red Tears	4,910
CESAREWITCH	Newmarket	Grey of Falloden	5,030
HORRIS HILL	Newbury	Foothill	4,226

1965

| ST LEGER | Doncaster | Provoke | 42,431 |

1967

| CHESTER CUP | Chester | Mahbub Aly | 4,749 |
| ROYAL LODGE | Ascot | Remand | 4,526 |

1970

| MIDDLE PARK | Newmarket | Brigadier Gerard | 10,515 |

1971

TWO THOUSAND GUINEAS	Newmarket	Brigadier Gerard	27,283
LADBROKE TRIAL	Lingfield	Homeric	4,886
COVENTRY STAKES	Royal Ascot	Sun Prince	5,393
ST JAMES'S PALACE STAKES	Royal Ascot	Brigadier Gerard	4,857
WM HILL GOLD TROPHY	Doncaster	Charlton	4,804
RICHMOND STAKES	Goodwood	Sallust	6,881
SUSSEX STAKES	Goodwood	Brigadier Gerard	12,134
QUEEN ELIZABETH II STAKES	Royal Ascot	Brigadier Gerard	5,761
CHAMPION STAKES	Newmarket	Brigadier Gerard	25,276

1972

LOCKINGE STAKES	Newbury	Brigadier Gerard	7,249
DIOMED STAKES	Epsom	Sallust	5,547
PRINCE OF WALES	Royal Ascot	Brigadier Gerard	8,221
ST JAMES'S PALACE STAKES	Royal Ascot	Sun Prince	8,422
ECLIPSE	Sandown	Brigadier Gerard	32,579
KING GEORGE VI AND QUEEN ELIZABETH	Ascot	Brigadier Gerard	60,202
SUSSEX STAKES	Goodwood	Sallust	12,033
PETER HASTINGS	Newbury	Colum	4,003

105

QUEEN ELIZABETH II	Ascot	Brigadier Gerard	£5,658
CHAMPION STAKES	Newmarket	Brigadier Gerard	35,048

1973

CLERICAL MEDICAL GREENHAM	Newbury	Boldboy	6,428
QUEEN ANNE	Royal Ascot	Sun Prince	4,023
EXTEL HANDICAP	Goodwood	Cupid	8,229
GREAT VOLTIGEUR	York	Buoy	6,161
AUTUMN CUP	Newbury	Sunyboy	4,901
WILLIAM HILL TROPHY	Sandown	Admetus	4,110

1974

ONE THOUSAND GUINEAS	Newmarket	Highclere	35,494
LADBROKE DERBY TRIAL	Lingfield	Bustino	7,728
DAVID DIXON GOLD CUP	York	Kinglet	4,070
YORKSHIRE CUP	York	Buoy	5,668
LOCKINGE	Newbury	Boldboy	16,650
CORONATION CUP	Epsom	Buoy	14,204
PRINCESS OF WALES	Newmarket	Buoy	4,090
JULY STAKES	Newmarket	Auction Ring	8,405
GREAT VOLTIGEUR	York	Bustino	6,636
ST LEGER	Doncaster	Bustino	56,766

1975

YORKSHIRE CUP	York	Riboson	7,125
CORONATION CUP	Epsom	Bustino	14,465
KING EDWARD VII STAKES	Royal Ascot	Sea Anchor	9,789
KING GEORGE STAKES	Goodwood	Auction Ring	6,040

1976

ORMONDE STAKES	Chester	Zimbalon	4,948
HENRY II STAKES	Sandown	Sea Anchor	7,052
BRITANNIA	Royal Ascot	Strabo	4,828
PRINCESS OF WALES	Newmarket	Smuggler	10,372
JULY STAKES	Newmarket	Sky Ship	10,824
JOHN SMITH MAGNET CUP	York	Bold Pirate	8,469
STRATHCLYDE STAKES	Ayr	Fife and Drum	4,204
GORDON STAKES	Goodwood	Smuggler	7,893
DONCASTER CUP	Doncaster	Sea Anchor	8,978

1977

DUKE OF YORK	York	Boldboy	9,758
WHITE ROSES	Newbury	Tully	5,635
LOCKINGE STAKES	Newbury	Relkino	17,034
THE OAKS	Epsom	Dunfermline	48,515
BENSON AND HEDGES GOLD CUP	York	Relkino	52,090
ST LEGER	Doncaster	Dunfermline	52,867
VERNONS SPRINT CUP	Haydock	Boldboy	18,895

1978

LADBROKE CRAVEN STAKES	Newmarket	Admiral's Launch	£6,552
WARREN STAKES	Epsom	Duke of Normandy	4,389
PRETTY POLLY STAKES	Newmarket	Upper Deck	4,752
YORKSHIRE CUP	York	Smuggler	14,272
HENRY II STAKES	Sandown	Smuggler	8,686
BASS CLUBMAN HANDICAP	Haydock	Homing	9,671
CHESTERS STAKES	Newcastle	Bolide	4,064
ROSE OF LANCASTER STAKES	Haydock	Cottage Pie	5,293
CHILD STAKES	Newmarket	Cistus	9,600
JOHN SMITH'S MAGNET CUP	York	Town and Country	9,968
LANSON CHAMPAGNE	Goodwood	Troy	6,721
GERRARD COUPE AUX BIJOUX	Goodwood	Town and Country	8,077
NASSAU	Goodwood	Cistus	14,256
GARROWBY LIMITED H'CAP	York	Rhyme Royal	7,067
HOLSTEN PILSNER	Doncaster	Town and Country	7,041
QUEEN ELIZABETH II STAKES	Ascot	Homing	12,880

BEST RACECOURSES

Newbury	104	wins
Newmarket	89	,,
Bath	73	,,
Ascot	62	,,
Sandown	51	,,
Salisbury	50	,,
Goodwood	47	,,
York	42	,,
Ripon	38	,,
Lingfield	37	,,

JOCKEYS

Joe Mercer	536	wins
Willie Carson	140	,,

In 1978 the only other jockeys to ride winners for him were: M. Wigham (1), Taffy Thomas (3), Joe Storrar (1) and B. Procter (1).

BEST MONTHS

July	193	wins
August	178	,,
June	174	,,
September	150	,,
May	129	,,

MULTIPLE WINS

His first four-timer, all at Newbury, was on 22nd September 1978. He has had 17 trebles and 130 doubles. The remarkable fact is the number of doubles, trebles and the four-timer which have been on one racecourse— no fewer than 1 four-timer, 8 trebles and 76 doubles. This is the highest proportion we can find. Of these, he had 12 doubles at Newbury, 11 at Bath and 9 at Newmarket.

OWNERS

Hern has trained for three successive principal owners: Major L. B. Halliday 1958–62, Lord Astor and J. J. Astor 1963 on, and Sir Michael Sobell and relatives from 1977.

Principal winning owners are: Major L. B. Halliday (184 wins), Mr J. J. Astor (151), Sir Michael Sobell (110), Lady Beaverbrook (85), Lord Rotherwick (76) and H.M. The Queen (63).

HORSES

Few of his horses win races for him for more than three seasons. Notable exceptions: Grey of Falloden (1963–7), Mahbub Aly (1963–7), Dashing (1964–9), and Burleigh (1974–8).

TWO-YEAR-OLDS

His first two-year-old winner in 1978 was Bolide at Bath on 24th April. Although his two-year-olds are not usually early, he has had several winners in March and April.

GENERAL

A remarkable record in the very big races. It is surprising that he has not yet won the Derby. Though he drew a blank at Royal Ascot in 1977 and 1978, he has won 15 races there:

RIBBLESDALE	1958
CHESHAM	1962, 1975
QUEEN ALEXANDRA	1965, 1974
QUEEN'S VASE	1967
COVENTRY	1971
ST JAMES'S PALACE	1971, 1972
PRINCE OF WALES	1972
QUEEN ANNE	1973
KING GEORGE V	1973, 1975
KING EDWARD VII	1975
BRITANNIA	1976

His English Classic tally to end of 1977 is three St Legers, one Two Thousand Guineas, one One Thousand Guineas and one Oaks.

108

Barry Hills

of South Bank, Lambourn

Barrington ('Barry') William Hills completed ten seasons as a trainer in the autumn of 1978. His rise to fame was so fast that I am tempted to call it instantaneous.

His first season at South Bank, Lambourn, once the home of Keith Piggott and his son Lester, was in 1969. He moved in during Houghton Week 1968 and the greatest challenge of his life began.

It was then that he graduated from many years as an apprentice, travelling head lad and head lad to the position of boss, a licensed trainer with its legion responsibilities, anxieties, problems of cash flow—and happily, when things go well, its short but rewarding periods of success and public acclaim.

Barry, whose father Bill was a fine head man with an outstandingly skilful and effective way with horses, was born in a Worcestershire nursing home, on 2nd April 1937. He was thirty-two when he trained his first winner, La Dolce Vita, at Thirsk on 18th April 1969. The filly was ridden by a young jockey beginning to make his name, Ernie Johnston. He has ridden for the stable ever since and, as seems fitting, he was on Barry's first classic winner, Enstone Spark (35 to 1), in the 1978 One Thousand Guineas.

Thus the 1969 season, Barry's first, had only been going 'five minutes', before this slightly built young man with a capacity for work, a facility for learning his craft and endowed with a quiet determination, had taken his first publicly witnessed step towards the top.

Having watched Barry's career over ten years and having known him for many more, I, as an observer of the Turf scene, cannot get away from his amazing progress. There was no spluttering, crawling and stalling in Barry's beginnings. He was in gear and on his way when others might be wondering if the lights had really changed. He had seventeen winners in his first year. Not bad, not at all bad, when we realise that he moved into South Bank, for which he paid £15,000, with only ten yearlings.

Apart from the obvious enterprise and industry of the man, what was it that enabled Barry to make the big step from head lad to public trainer with such alacrity?

The straight answer to that is a few successful bets. Some luck as well, but I am an earnest supporter of the belief that God helps those who help themselves. Barry certainly did that. Let him tell you in his own words just what happened:

'I was travelling head lad for John Oxley at Newmarket. Well, we didn't have an argument for eight years. Then we did have one and I thought well, if that's the way it is, I want to go on my own.

'I had won quite a bit of money on Frankincense in the 1968 Lincoln.' (This very useful horse, trained for Lady Halifax by John Oxley, carried 9 st 8 lb to victory and started at 100 to 8. He is currently successful at stud.) 'I had also backed some good winners in the previous year,' Barry went on. 'A few of us travelling head lads got together. We didn't bet big but we had some yankees and cross doubles. We more or less cleaned up in our small way.'

Then Barry named some of the other winners which enabled him to raise £15,000 to buy South Bank with its twenty-four boxes and which now has eighty-one.

Ovaltine, 100 to 8 winner of the Johnnie Walker Ebor Handicap in 1967 and the Goodwood Cup (5 to 2) the following year, was one. Lacquer's 1967 20 to 1 win in the Cambridgeshire, and the

Checking the day's training schedule: Barry Hills with his head lad Snowy Outen. On the left is 17-year-old Tommy Glynn, who used to ride Hickleton. (Keystone)

Peter Payne-Gallwey trained Sky Diver, winner of Goodwood's Stewards Cup in 1967 (20 to 1) and 1968 (100 to 6), added to Barry's capital, eventually put to such good use.

Once Barry had fired his first warning shot with La Dolce Vita, indicating that he would soon be in the thick of the struggle for winners, he began to build up his stable. Let him tell us something of this:

'I bought Gay Perch in my first year for around £1,000. He won four races for us in 1969. La Dolce Vita cost me under £200. Not only was she my first winner but she improved my score shortly afterwards by winning a seller at Wolverhampton. We bought her in for £1,000.

'Then there was an American bred called Texanitania. We bought him through Willie Carson from Mimi Van Cutsem, whose husband Bernard, as you know, died in the middle of a fine career as a trainer. Texanitania was bought for Mr S. Lee who lived at Southport. He wanted to have a bit of a touch so we gave this three-year-old his first run in a six furlong maiden at Thirsk. A month later, ridden by Willie Carson, he won a mile maiden at Ripon at 10 to 1.'

What could be better for a young trainer? It sounds so easy but as many a racing man or woman knows, it most certainly is not. Barry, like a great golf professional or champion snooker player, has a way of making his strokes appear as easy as turning on the telly.

We have had a taste of the good things to come in Barry's training career. Before we become fully involved with this let us turn back to his early days.

Here again let Barry tell the story in his own words, which now and then carry that pleasant 'burr' of Gloucestershire which I know well, having worked there as a young man and served as a Territorial soldier in the County Regiment.

'My father, Bill, was head lad with old Tom Rimell, father of Fred, at Kinnersley, Worcestershire, for twelve years. He had the National winner Forbra at that time and other good winners such as Teme Willow and Tit Willow. He also had a spell when he

112

trained ponies at Fareham, Hampshire and turned out Mountain Cloud to win the Northolt Derby.

'Father came from Nottingham and served his apprenticeship with Sam Pickering, at Kennet, near Newmarket. Then he was with "Dasher" Dale and old man Goby. He rode winners over fences and hurdles before he became head lad with Tom Rimell.

'I was born in 1937 and we went to live in Quedgeley, five miles outside Gloucester on the A38. When the war was over, Father, who had been out of racing because of ill health, wanted to go back into the game. I was nine years old, mad on my pony, the countryside and farming but not very mad on school. My father then went to that fine trainer George Colling as head lad. So we all, including my pony Polly, went off to Newmarket. I can remember it so well, particularly going to St Mary's School in the Fordham-road opposite Tom Thomson Jones's place. Yes, I can remember it all right because in 1947 we had the worst snowfalls and coldest winter for years. It went on and on.'

This weather could not have helped Bill Hills because after a couple of years with George Colling he contracted tuberculosis and the Hills family moved back to Gloucestershire, to Upton-on-Severn where Barry's mother came from. 'Our roots were there,' said Barry.

It was while Hills senior was with George Colling that young Barry used to ride Polly out with the First Lot of horses at exercise and then go to school. Those were the days when comedian Vic Oliver's Voluntary did well for the stable, which was also well supported by the Ostrers, members of the film industry.

When Barry was reluctantly continuing his schooling at Upton-on-Severn he used somehow to ride out quite often for Fred Rimell at Kinnersley.

Fred eventually took Barry on as an apprentice and the boy, aged thirteen, had his first ride on Golden Chance II at the now defunct Birmingham racecourse, a good track in not very beautiful surroundings. Incidentally it was here that I remember being a commentator in what was, I think, the first evening racing programme broadcast by Independent Television in the mid 1950s.

'I remember my first ride vividly,' Barry told me. 'I was drawn between Gordon Richards and Michael Beary so I was in the very best company. There were a lot of runners and both these jockeys kept shouting at me to keep straight. I rode this horse several times in races in my early teens.'

Barry continued to work with Fred Rimell, one of the great professionals of our time, who at that period was winning races with Land Fort, Old Mortality, Victory Light, Coloured Schoolboy, Unconditional Surrender and Steel Courage.

The young Barrington Hills learned plenty at Kinnersley but he hankered after flat racing. Fred had only a few runners on the Flat and Barry thought he was missing something. Fred suggested that he should go to Ron Smyth at Epsom but Hills senior advocated George Colling, his old boss, at Newmarket and there Barry went.

Barry rode seven or eight winners with George Colling including four on Peter Pan before he had to do his National Service. In this he was lucky in that he got a good job : Regimental Sergeant Major's Horse Holder in the King's Troop, the Royal Horse Artillery. He reckons he was even luckier in that he was discharged after only eight months and two days of musical rides and twenty-one gun salutes!

Hills senior was very ill and Barry was released on compassionate grounds. Gunner Hills left the Army in September and took over the job of travelling head lad with George Colling that winter.

'When I was apprenticed to George Colling I looked after Acropolis,' Barry told me. 'He was a very good horse but he used to put his stifle out. When he was third in the Derby behind Phil Drake in 1955 he wasn't fit because he went wrong after the Newmarket Stakes and his preparation was messed up. He was an unlucky horse. Don't forget he was a brother of Alycidon, a tremendous stayer and half-brother to another good horse, Borealis.'

Many people still have the impression that Alycidon was not a fast horse. In fact he could gallop with great speed but he did not accelerate well. It took him time to work up to his top pace.

114

Some of Barry Hills' string at Lambourn on the way to the gallops.
(Peckham's of Stroud)

Acropolis was a much better quickener. Barry said: 'I remember him galloping as a two-year-old with Mr Richard Stanley's very useful three-year-old filly Holwood, by Umidwar, out of Beausite. She couldn't get away from him. He was a very good horse. His best distance was, in my view, a mile and a quarter.'

Then Barry reminded me of something: 'Acropolis broke the course record at Newmarket on his own, you know, when he had only one rival in the Newmarket Stakes. That was Lord Rosebery's Rowland Ward. He ran off the course.' Acropolis clocked 2 min 4.54 sec which, to the best of my belief, was not a record but it was very fast indeed.

George Colling, younger brother of Jack whom Dick Hern followed at West Ilsley, was an extremely honourable and kindly man. He trained Nimbus to win the Guineas (beating Abernant) and the Derby in 1949, and a score of other top class horses.

His health, which gave him cause for anxiety over the years, finally broke down in 1959 and he died in a Bournemouth hospital, aged fifty-five, on 18th April, the day that Mr Dick Hollingsworth's good mare, Cutter, which George had trained, won the John Porter Stakes at Newbury. John Oxley was then standing in for George as trainer. This young man who had been an assistant for a short time then took over many of the horses trained previously by George.

I mention George Colling at some length because it was this thorough, highly respected man, who helped to train Barry Hills in the ways of handling racehorses and men. Barry said of him, 'We knew he was not a well man but he was always most methodical and an absolute gentleman to work for. He was completely dedicated to his job. He worked his horses progressively up. He did not hurry them and was, in fact, extremely patient. I probably learned a lot from him and I know I try to do as I think he would when I'm faced with certain situations.'

Before John Oxley went to help George Colling he had a couple of seasons with Geoffrey Brooke. He had only been a few months with George before, as Barry put it, John was 'chucked in at the deep end'. He had to take full responsibility almost too quickly. He turned out plenty of winners but he retired from the training game as a comparatively young man. Barry learned much from his contacts with both these trainers.

By 1968 Barry was ripe for a trainer's job. He was intelligent and experienced in several important aspects of the calling he contemplated. Above all he had an asset, the lack of which often prevents many a likely man from becoming a successful trainer— he had capital. Not much, but enough. He was not chucked in at the deep end of the training business. He dived in and struck out strongly with confidence derived from experience. He knew what to do when faced with problems.

*　　*　　*

Bill Hills, Barry's father, had a priceless knack with horses. Unless the case was hopeless he could always get a horse right. George Colling and Charlie Pratt, from that fine family of horsemen to which Lester Piggott is related through his mother, greatly appreciated this art during the comparatively short time that Hills senior served them. Barry is strongly of the opinion that his father would have trained successfully but for ill health. Tuberculosis brought about the removal of one lung. Unhappily Bill's other lung was also affected. Were he alive he would be proud of his son's rapid progress in his profession.

Looking at the eight men in this book it is fascinating to observe how they have arrived in the top echelon of trainers. Some have had the benefit of good education and spent their childhood in homes of comparative affluence. Others, including Barry, have come up the hard way. He lived with the rattle of buckets and the clatter of hooves in stable yards where his father worked. Schooling at times was non-existent but in the end in so far as Barry is concerned it doesn't seem to matter. He has poise and confidence. He is capable of holding his own in the racing world at any level. Money and what I suppose I had best call a privileged upbringing are together far from being an unobstructed motorway to success. Without self control and commercial prudence they can precipitate the saddest and most disastrous failures, of which I have seen some in a lifetime associated with the Turf. I am happy to say that of the eight good men and true featured in this book all have had their share of good luck and some may have much more to come and others rather less but all have this in common—they are dedicated. When younger they took off their coats—and, to use an ugly but expressive phrase, 'got stuck in'. All of them are still capable of that—should the situation demand it!

Barry remembers with warmth those horses which helped to carry him along towards success. 'There was Golden Monad,' he told me. 'He went through the first season without winning and towards the back-end was fourth with 7 st 1 lb in the Criterion Nursery, at Newmarket, won by Karoo, ridden by Willie Carson, and trained by Bernard Van Cutsem. Well, Golden Monad won the Prix Henry Delamarre, worth £11,742, at Longchamp the next year and was my first winner abroad.'

Hickleton, by Exbury out of Fan Light, by Wilwyn, was one of the horses which helped make Barry. He was going round John Oxley's horses one April evening with Lady Halifax when she remarked when they were in Hickleton's box, 'If ever a horse needs a mile and a quarter now, he does'. Events were to prove that Barry knew what the Countess was talking about. John Oxley won with this chestnut as a three-year-old. Barry, by then no longer employed by John, bought him out of a mile-and-a-half seller at Newmarket in August. He was not at that meeting but the horse was purchased by Mr R. Dawson, on Barry's strong recommendation, for £500—a maiden bid. He was Barry's

One of Barry Hills' early triumphs: Hickleton, ridden by Ernie Johnson, winning the Great Met at Epsom from Kutch (Tony Murray). (Sport & General)

first big winner. Next year he won the Great Metropolitan and was then beaten a head in the Chester Cup by Altogether, ridden by Walter Bentley. Barry reckons Hickleton should have won. 'Should have trotted up,' he said, 'but he had an unlucky run.'

In his second year Barry had a two-year-old called Hot Potato, winner of several races. He was also successful with Close Combat, Kellac and Trasi Girl, dam of Trasi's Son, by Pretendre, the colt on which Paul Cook so nearly won the Derby. Trasi Girl won the National Stakes at Sandown. Hickleton won the Brown Jack Stakes (2¾ m) at Ascot in July. 'We won thirty-two races and £37,000 in stakes including that race in France. We were really off the mark,' said Barry.

Barry's third year, 1971, was, as he put it, 'The year Henry Zeisel came into the game'.

'I met him,' recalled Barry, 'in a box at Royal Ascot. He told me he would like to buy a horse in October and he would spend £3,000. He wrote one of the very few letters he has ever sent to me, enclosing a cheque for £1,500, deposit for the horse. I went to the sales and bought him Rheingold . . .'

Yes, Rheingold. Just like that. It sounded as if he had casually popped round the corner and bought a box of cigars (which, incidentally, he enjoys). Barry gently reminded me : 'Rheingold won £365,000 in stakes and was syndicated for £1,000,000.'

So, the one-time little boy who had been apprenticed to Fred Rimell and George Colling; the slightly built little scamp who played truant from school rather more than is generally tolerated, was approaching the centre of the stage in only his third year as a trainer. He has not been far removed from it ever since.

In 1971 other horses too kept the Hills star high. The chestnut Hickleton won the Queen Alexandra Stakes easily and also won at Haydock. The same year, Meaden (Barry's first runner in the Derby) won at Deauville. He followed this with his third winner abroad when Mr and Mrs Sonny Enfield's Our Mirage won the Prix de Salamandre, worth £15,639.

Rheingold won a maiden 6 f event at Newcastle on 28th August worth around £800. He was then runner-up to Crowned Prince in the Champagne Stakes at Doncaster and the Dewhurst Stakes at

Newmarket. Lord Porchester's Disguise won the Horris Hill. Hickleton kept on winning and Galiano was coming into play. 'By the end of my third year I had won £46,000 and had thirty-nine winners including five abroad of which two were at Ostend,' Barry told me.

'Rheingold boosted the whole business tremendously,' Barry went on. 'He was a very, very good horse but if he was just a bit weak, a bit off-colour, he could run a really bad race. He would improve with the weather. He came to top pitch around mid-summer. Obviously the older he got the stronger he became.'

I asked whether Rheingold had a smooth Derby preparation. Barry replied: 'I always rated Rheingold inferior to Our Mirage at the time. Between the Dante Stakes which he won at York in May 1972 and the Derby, Rheingold improved by stones. You

Lester Piggott has good reason to smile after his 1973 Arc de Triomphe win on Rheingold.

could see it out at exercise each day, how much he was coming on. He was beaten a short head in the Derby by Roberto but he was a much better horse the day he won the Grand Prix de St Cloud. He hacked up.

'Rheingold had every chance in the Derby. Ernie Johnson rode a super race on him. In my opinion he rode a far better race on him than when he won the Derby on Blakeney in 1969. I think he handled Rheingold marvellously. I expect you realised that the colt did not act properly on the course. We simply had to run him in the Derby although we already knew from the way he performed in the Blue Riband Trial Stakes in which he was fourth to Scottish Rifle that he didn't really "go a yard" on the track.' A fully excusable and understandable exaggeration on Barry's part particularly when considered in the light of Rheingold's five-length win not long after Epsom in the £47,224 Grand Prix de St Cloud.

'Of course Rheingold has got to be the best horse I've trained, so far. He beat Allez France by three lengths in the Arc de Triomphe (1973). She won it in 1974.

'Going back a bit—Rheingold was second to Dahlia in the King George VI and Queen Elizabeth Stakes, and Our Mirage which had run fourth in the Derby, was third. Then he was fourth in that graveyard race—the Benson and Hedges Gold Cup at York won by Roberto. After that Rheingold didn't run before the Arc but I kept him going.'

Barry then made a statement which revealed the great importance he attached to his decision to keep Rheingold 'ticking over'.

'It was one of the best things I have ever done in my life with horses,' he went on, 'for, you see, he had been quite busy and wanted building up again. I hate letting horses down—giving them virtually nothing to do. Of course you can give a horse a rest but you must keep the wheels turning. This I did with Rheingold and he just built up and regained his strength He came right back for the Arc.'

The veteran trainer Sid Mercer, one of the truly expert horse handlers of my time, was, at this period, a wise counsellor to Barry who told me: 'Sid came down and helped me a bit with Rheingold. He prescribed some of his powders for the horse and I am sure they were beneficial. Sid was a great man and a great horseman. I owe a lot to him for his advice, particularly at that period.'

Such names as Galiano, winner of Ascot's Joe Coral Victoria Cup (that fine seven-furlong sprint which began its life at now defunct Hurst Park), Avon Valley, Spirit in the Sky and Our Mirage tripped off Barry's tongue as he reviewed his earlier years. Our Mirage, of the same vintage as Rheingold, was, as we have seen, overshadowed by him. Not only did he run extremely well just behind his stable companion but he also won the coveted Dee Stakes (one of Barry's specialities) and the more valuable Great Voltigeur Stakes, York's St Leger Trial.

Then along came Lt. Col. I. Chandos-Pole's Proverb, another good horse. He won the Chester Vase (1973) and the Goodwood and Doncaster Cups in the following year and was runner-up to Ragstone in the Ascot Gold Cup. Barry topped up his bubbling cup of success with: 'Hickleton won the Prix Gladiateur, and Rheingold won his second Grand Prix de St Cloud. In fact up to that time the value of the races we won on the Continent came to only about £20,000 less than that won by every other winner I had trained at home.'

Now came a testing time for our crest-of-a-wave trainer. He had to make a big decision. So quickly and effectively had he established himself that his reputation was made. His success was not the outcome of ephemeral virtuosity but sustained and inspired. In the same way that the services of a leading teenage apprentice are sought by the big battalions in racing, Barry's too, were sought—but twenty years later in life than with the boy wonders of the Turf.

'I was offered the job as trainer to Daniel Wildenstein in France,' he told me. 'I turned it down. It would have meant moving and what with the alterations and additions here plus the way things were going I just didn't want to go. Anyhow one of my terms was that I should take ten horses from my string here. They wouldn't stand for that. Their plan was that I should follow Albert Klimscha. Well, as you know, Angel Penna got the job.'

Barry then glanced again at his record book and reminded me

122

that in 1972 the stable won £109,000 and 57 races including two in France. 'We also had 59 seconds and 48 thirds—so we were right on target,' said Barry. The following year, 1973, his record read : 62 winners, 62 seconds and 36 thirds. The winners brought in £325,000. This was the year of Rheingold's second Grand Prix de St Cloud. He also won the John Porter Stakes at Newbury and the Hardwicke Stakes at Royal Ascot. Dragonara Palace, owned by Mrs Cyril Stein, wife of Ladbroke's boss, captured the historic July Stakes for two-year-olds, at Newmarket, and also the Richmond Stakes at Goodwood. Straight as a Die won Ascot's Royal Lodge Stakes and Our Mirage picked up the Jockey Club Stakes at Newmarket.

1974 was Dibidale's year. Barry is unlikely to forget this for several reasons all of which are woven into the story he told me about her. She will be remembered by most followers of racing as a filly who needed plenty of give in the ground and an unlucky loser of the Oaks.

Barry told me, 'We started off with Jack Stallard's Galiano winning the Joe Coral Victoria Cup and then came Dibidale and the Oaks. She had only run twice as a two-year-old, showing promise each time. She fully confirmed this by beating Mil's Bomb by seven lengths in the Cheshire Oaks in May.

'I can remember vividly Nick Robinson who owned Dibidale being at Epsom the day before the Oaks. We were dejected because it had not rained and although the ground was not bad we wanted it softer. We decided to leave her in the race but were most unlikely to run her unless the ground eased considerably. I had a horse called Danum, winner of several races, running at Haydock that night. I was going to fly up with Ernie Johnson so I suggested to Nick that he should come up with us and go to Haydock. Well, glad to say, he did and we won the first race with Mrs Keaveney's Danum at 4 to 1. Robert Sangster who was steward at Haydock won the fifth race with Puritan (10 to 1) and then asked us to supper in the Stewards' room after the last race. We all stayed the night with Robert and had a right few jars to drown our Epsom sorrows.

'About three o'clock in the morning I woke up and heard the

Dibidale after winning the 1974 Irish Guineas Oaks at The Curragh, accompanied by Barry Hills.

rain beating at the window. I couldn't sleep any more because I was wondering if it was raining at Epsom. I got up and rang home to ask what the weather was doing. It was raining here at Lambourn so we rang someone at Epsom as early as we decently could. There was good news—it had rained all night. We flew south and decided to run the filly.

'Well! We should have won by five lengths. As you'll remember she lost her weight cloth during the race and was disqualified. She beat the same animals very easily a few days later in the Irish Guineas Oaks on faster ground than at Epsom.

'Anyone to blame? I don't think so. She was saddled properly and this was checked at the start. They couldn't fine me or anything like that. Mind you, I know what happened. She jumped a path at the top of the hill. In doing so she stretched right out and, as it were, tended to jump through her girths.'

124

That Dibidale tragedy—she finished third with a slipped saddle, no weight cloth and Willie Carson riding bare back—was Polygamy's happy chance. One man's meat, another man's poison : Peter Walwyn thus took the Oaks with Mr Louis Freedman's little filly, originally trained for the One Thousand Guineas in which she was unlucky according to Peter.

Dibidale, by Aggressor out of Priddy Maid, then won (£24,032) in Ireland and followed this up by winning the £13,872 Yorkshire Oaks by a neck from Mil's Bomb, her old Chester rival.

Next season Dibidale had four races before lining up for the £8,098 Geoffrey Freer Stakes at Newbury on 16th August. She started third favourite of ten at 11 to 2. Halfway through the race she broke her off foreleg at the fetlock. The winner was Consol, trained by Peter Walwyn.

'We tried desperately to save her,' Barry told me. 'We got her back here and she lived for another three weeks. She had so many anaesthetics and operations. They knocked hell out of her. We had to put her down. It was the only thing to do.

'After she had been put down we examined the damaged fetlock joint and leg. I'll tell you this : If you had hit an oyster with a ten pound hammer you could not have found so many pieces as there were in Dibidale's smashed joint. It was just like a box of matches.'

Dibidale is buried in the garden at South Bank. (Fiona Vigors)

125

Not long after this sad reminder of the end of a talented filly Barry took me on to the newly mown grass on the sunny slope of his garden, between the house and the narrow old road below which winds with the little river on its lazy, beautiful way to Newbury. There on that green hillside is a simple tombstone such as can be found in churchyards throughout the land. Beneath this one are the remains of Dibidale whose luck went to extremes. We stood there for two or three minutes. Barry probably for the thousandth, and I for the first time, just thinking of this filly and of what was, and what might have been.

As I write, Dibidale's dam, Priddy Maid (by Acropolis), now dead, can be represented on the Turf by only two more offspring : Robert Sangster's Etre, a three-year-old filly by Green God, and Cracaval, a two-year-old colt by Mount Hagen, last foal of the dam. He is owned in partnership by Robert Sangster, Nick Robinson and others.

1974 also saw four wins for Mr J. Ketteley's consistent and smart two-year-old Royal Manacle, beaten a neck by Steel Heart in the William Hill Middle Park Stakes. This colt, winner the next season of the Thirsk Classic Trial, helped swell Barry's 1974 total of winners to sixty-five.

Although Lord Ranfurly's Stand to Reason won Goodwood's £13,872 Richmond Stakes and Charles St George's Marco Ricci took the £5,192 Redcar Gold Trophy in 1975, the year is best remembered by Barry for the victories of the hardy and consistent fillies, Mrs Charles Radclyffe's three-year-old Duboff, winner of nine races, and Mr Kalifa Sasi's two-year-old Nagwa, winner of thirteen races that year including one in Mr A. Fathaly's name.

Among Duboff's 1975 triumphs were the Extel Handicap at Goodwood and the Sun Chariot Stakes at Newmarket. She also won Newmarket's Child Stakes in 1976. 'Duboff was a tough filly,' commented Barry. 'You could pull her out any day of the week and run her.' She was by So Blessed, out of Proper Pretty by Worden II. She won eleven races from seven to ten furlongs as a three- and four-year-old. She was unbeaten as a three-year-old in England when she won nine races.

Nagwa, a brown filly, by Tower Walk, out of Tamarisk Way,

was a two-year-old wonder of the decade. She won thirteen races, and was only out of the frame once in her twenty public appearances. She did not break her duck until winning at Leicester (5 f) on 14th June, her fourth start. After that she won at Brighton (5 f) 23rd June, Haydock (6 f) 5th July, Redcar (5 f) 16th July, Chepstow (5 f) 25th August, Pontefract (6 f) 1st September, Thirsk (5 f) 6th September, Folkestone (5 f) 10th September, Redcar (7 f) 27th September, York (6 f) 11th October, Catterick (6 f) 18th October, Leicester (6 f) 20th October, and Lingfield (7 f) 3rd November. Willie Carson and Ernie Johnson won on her in the first half of the season but from Chepstow, 25th August, the apprentice Raymond Cochrane took over and the partnership was successful nine times. Incidentally when I checked this hardy filly's victories in the index of Races Past, 1975, the Jockey Club's official record, I could only make her winning total twelve. Winning references in this superb volume are given in parenthesis. Somehow the brackets were omitted from race 1658 which was Nagwa's win at Haydock on 5th July. I mention this index error with humility knowing, as a writer on Turf matters, how easy it is to perpetrate and perpetuate mistakes.

'Apart from being tough she coped with all sorts of going,' was Barry's simple comment on this remarkable filly who with Duboff won twenty-two races in 1975 and accounted for more than a quarter of their trainer's total eighty-one victories in that season.

Looking at Barry's records in the last few years we can understand why people are inclined to say that he is a specialist handler of fillies. He admits, as he must, that he has done well with them, but says he can do just as well with the other sex if the great unseen power who controls our fortunes deals him the right sort of yearling colts out of the pack. When we are faced with the names of Dibidale, Duboff, Nagwa, Mofida, and Durtal it is understandable why Barry has been 'typed'. His last pronouncement to me on this subject was: 'Most of my early big winners were colts. It's just a question of running fast—as simple as that.'

We come now to 1976—when Robert Sangster's bay filly Durtal, by Lyphard (USA), out of Derma II, by Sunny Boy, made such an impression. She won three of her five races being narrowly beaten

127

by Icena in York's Lowther Stakes (fillies) and defeated by four lengths by the colt J. O. Tobin, in Doncaster's Laurent Perrier Champagne Stakes.

'Durtal is a very, very good filly,' he said. 'If I had the chance to train her again as a two- and three-year-old I would give her a completely different programme. I ran her over five furlongs first time out and then over six furlongs. I wanted to run her in the Criterium des Pouliches which is over a mile at Longchamp in October. However, Lester wanted to ride her in the six furlong Cheveley Park at Newmarket. He jumped her off, made all the running and won (£34,426).'

That was a marvellous prize to win but Barry hankers after the idea that he ought to have made a top class miler or one-and-a-quarter-mile animal out of her. He believes he could have done this if the filly had not been trained and raced as a sprinter as a juvenile. As a three-year-old she won Newbury's £5,271 Fred Darling Stakes (7 f) in a canter and dead-heated for second place in the Poule d'Essai des Pouliches, the French One Thousand Guineas (1 m).

Mr Kalifa Sasi's Right Tack filly, Mofida (out of Wold Lass, by Vilmorin), moved into vision in 1976. She won five races and was placed eight times in fifteen outings. Her most valuable win as a juvenile was £4,010 when she carried 9 st 2 lb in the Firth of Clyde Stakes 6 f at Ayr in September. Her best wins in 1977 were the £7,140 William Hill Trophy at York and the Sporting Chronicle Handicap of £4,097 at Haydock. 'Mofida doesn't quite get seven furlongs,' Barry told me, 'and she needs a cut in the ground to produce her best.'

Barry had sixty winners in 1976. He followed this with seventy-six winners of £140,000 in stakes in 1977. His horses also collected £61,000 in second money and he was fourth in the trainers' list. Among the stars of '77 not so far mentioned were

After making all the running, Durtal comes out of the dip to win Newmarket's William Hill Cheveley Park Stakes. (Sport & General)

Lady Mere, winner of Epsom's Princess Elizabeth Stakes; Lord Helpus, winner of the Silver Jubilee at Kempton, and the £12,438 Princess of Wales Stakes at Newmarket; two-year-old Delta Sierra, winner of six races including the Cock of the North at Haydock; Matinale, the Ascot Stakes; Aloft, the Princess Royal Stakes at Ascot; and the stable's 1978 Derby hope Sexton Blake, winner of Newcastle's Seaton Delaval and Doncaster's Laurent Perrier Champagne Stakes of £13,810.

'I do not have many owners who breed their own yearlings. I buy ninety per cent of the horses,' Barry told me, 'and I buy them myself. I go round the sales. I spent more than £1,100,000 on yearlings in 1977 and I buy quite a few on spec. It's a worrying business—very hard on the cash flow. I really have to work to find owners for these horses.

'What I look for is a good walker, an active horse, not too heavy topped. I'm not giving you exact amounts but these are the approximate prices I paid for some very good animals: Duboff £9,000, Mofida £5,000, Sexton Blake £5,000, Rheingold £3,000 and Our Mirage £6,000.'

That is more than enough evidence to confirm that Barry is a good picker.

I asked my host if he chose these yearlings from the sales catalogues. His answer may be surprising to many.

'No,' he said, 'I never look at the catalogue. I go to the sales with the catalogue unopened. On the other hand I do acknowledge that pedigrees are important. What I do is to go round the yearlings in their boxes—just Pat Hogan, who is a private blood-stock agent, and myself. We see as many as we can. Then we start sorting them out. I go back and have another look at a horse that appealed to me. Then, and only then, do I look at the pedigree. What it boils down to is that I value the horse according to the pedigree, after I have seen it.

'As I've told you, I never look at the catalogue before I go to the sale but if someone rings me up and says "please have a look at lot number so and so" then of course I do so.'

*   *   *

130

Barry then paid tribute to some of his patrons who had helped, as he said, 'to put me on my feet'.

'Henry Zeisel helped me with Rheingold. That horse and I helped Henry in our turn,' smiled Barry. 'Henry has been good to me but he has never had many horses here. He has had his horses in several other stables. Robert Sangster has helped me tremendously, mostly with fillies like Durtal and Lady Mere. He sends the colts to Vincent O'Brien. Robert has twenty-five animals with me. He comes to see them once or twice a year but he sees plenty of them at the races.

'Keith Hsu has helped me a great deal and has stood by me. He comes from Hong Kong but lives here. He was "in" with Mofida and Nagwa. Nick Robinson and Sonny Enfield are others who have always been loyal supporters.'

One has only to look at published lists of Barry's patrons to realise how many do trust this comparatively young man, something of an inexhaustible comet flashing among the firmament of Turf stars.

If the reader has borne with me so far it will be realised that we have already had several good views of Barry's training methods, which he summed up with : 'I go by the horses. They'll tell you when they are ready. That was George Colling's way. I haven't been one to have early two-year-olds. Mine always seem to want three or four runs before they come to themselves. I do not try them at home. They do nice progressive work. If you started trying horses on these stiff Lambourn gallops you'd soon be in the workhouse.'

I cannot end this piece on Barry Hills without mentioning, as he would wish, some of those who apart from owners and trainers have helped him in his rapid rise to the top. He has had the backing of his family. He has four sons : John, rider of three winners in 1978, Michael, Richard and Charles. Barry remarried in 1977. His bride, Miss Penny Woodhouse, was a talented show jumping rider and is of the greatest help to Barry, although as I write she is fully occupied by looking after Charles Barrington, born on 28th September 1978, the day before Galaxy Libra, a promising two-year-old, won at Ascot.

Hawaiian Sound poses between Penny and Barry Hills. (Fiona Vigors)

Paddy Newsome, who died in 1978, was father of Barry's first wife. He was a sound jockey and, above all, a superb horseman and in earlier years was associated with the stable of Joe Lawson, who trained at Manton and Newmarket. Paddy worked for Barry and rode Rheingold and other good horses in all their work. 'He was,' said Barry, 'a truly marvellous work jockey.

'My head lad is Snowy Outen. He has been with me since I started training. Snowy was apprenticed at Egerton, Newmarket. He is a very loyal man. He was with the late Peter Hastings Bass at Kingsclere for about ten years and he had the same job with Peter Lowis who now has an executive job with Lambourn

Transport.' Others who are in charge of yards at South Bank are Hughie Heaney and Bill Troop. Bill breaks all the yearlings. 'They have all been with me for some years and are fine members of my team,' was how Barry summed them up.

The ex-jockey Ron Sheather used to be Barry's assistant but moved to Newmarket. His place at South Bank has been taken by Robert Williams since November 1977. The efficient and helpful girls in Barry's office are Veronica Telford who is the racing secretary, and Julia Hall, in charge of accounts.

Barry and his team rose to even greater heights in 1978 when Enstone Spark won the One Thousand Guineas and Hawaiian Sound captured the £49,200 Benson and Hedges Gold Cup and very nearly won two Derbys.

First the Enstone Spark story. A bay filly, bred by the William Hill Stud, she was not very big but, as Barry said, 'there was enough of her and she was strong'. She was by Sparkler, out of Laxmi, by Palestine. Sparkler was a very good miler trained by Sam Armstrong. This horse was twice runner-up to Brigadier Gerard and on one of those occasions when the going was soft got within inches of victory. Palestine won the Two Thousand Guineas. So it was not surprising that Enstone Spark, winner of four of her nine races as a two-year-old when trained by Richard Hannon, made the grade, just once and in a big way as a three-year-old.

Barry told me : 'The British Bloodstock Agency bought her at the end of her two-year-old season. When she was sent to me I liked her and she did awfully well through the winter. She was in the One Thousand Guineas and we decided to go for that. I was of the opinion that she would stay. Well, as you know, she went to Newmarket and beat Fair Salinia by a length and was not really extended. It was no surprise to me, I fancied her and backed her at thirty-five to one. Not a big bet but then you don't have to have much on to win quite a bit at those odds.'

This was the only time that she showed her real form as a three-year-old. According to Barry she might have won the Coronation Stakes at Royal Ascot but she got a slight knock on the turn into the straight when 'all four legs were off the ground, and that turned her over'. After that she seemed to lose her enthusiasm.

She was a tricky filly with no real vice but someone always had to walk behind her to get her on to the gallops. Owned by a Canadian, Mr R. Bonnycastle, she was destined to visit the Bold Ruler stallion Bold Forbes in America in 1979.

Hawaiian Sound, a bay colt, was bred by Mr A. B. Hancock III, in Kentucky, and raced in England by Mr Robert Sangster and a couple of partners. The colt, by Hawaii, out of Sound of Success, by Successor, showed quite enough form in his two-year-old races to give his trainer the view that he would make a good three-year-old.

'His last race in 1977 was the William Hill Futurity and he got a bad bump which put paid to his chance about two and a half furlongs out,' Barry recalled. As a three-year-old he soon won a couple of races and in one of these, at Newmarket, he beat M-Lolshan, winner later in the year of the Irish St Leger.

Barry was thinking what a good Derby prospect the colt was when he was beaten a neck by Icelandic in the Chester Vase run over a few yards more than the Derby distance. Barry began to wonder if he stayed the trip.

'After this Ernie Johnson decided to ride our other Derby colt Sexton Blake. Both Lester Piggott and Pat Eddery rode the colt at work before the Derby. Both turned down the offer of the ride at Epsom. After consultation with Mr Sangster and his partners we decided to go for Willie Shoemaker.'

There was no trouble in obtaining this maestro among American jockeys. He had expressed a desire to ride in Europe many times in the past.

'Basically I gave Shoemaker a free hand in the Derby,' Barry told me, 'I didn't really want him to make the running but looking back on it I think he rode a most marvellous race on the horse. Just as Lester can do, Shoemaker impressed his personality on the race and he had them all stacked up behind him like a pack of cards coming down Tattenham Hill. Shirley Heights just collared him and that was bad luck.

'In the Irish Sweeps Derby Shoemaker wanted to hold up the colt or at least drop him in behind the leaders. For some reason he let him run along and nothing left him alone. He kept on being taken on through the race and as you know he was only a head and a neck behind Shirley Heights and Exdirectory at the finish. Shoemaker came back very annoyed. He thought he had made a mess of it.'

Ridden by Lester Piggott the colt went on to beat Gunner B in the Benson and Hedges at York.

'In my view he was not such a good horse at York as when he ran in his Derbys,' said Barry, 'but in nearly all his races as a three-year-old he had top class time figures according to Mr Phil Bull's Timeform organisation.'

Hawaiian Sound may not have got a mile and a half as a three-year-old but as a four-year-old he may do so without trouble. At all events the programme which Barry envisaged for this colt in 1979 consisted mostly of races over a mile and a quarter or thereabouts and included the Earl of Sefton Stakes, the Prix Ganay, the Prince of Wales Stakes, the Eclipse, the Benson and Hedges Gold Cup, followed, if all went well, by a crack at the Arc de Triomphe over a mile and a half and 'at the end of the day' as Barry put it, a run in the Washington International on the way home to Keeneland and a stud career. Well, he will deserve that luxury and life of ease.

STATISTICAL RECORDS

Barry Hills has had 10 seasons as a trainer and 569 winners of £952,348 in first prize money on the Flat in Britain. He was in the top ten of trainers in only his fourth season and has remained there.

TRAINERS' TABLE

1972	10th	55 winners of	£52,628
1973	7th	62 winners of	£92,060
1974	7th	67 winners of	£87,596
1975	4th	81 winners of	£107,603
1976	7th	60 winners of	£113,180
1977	4th	76 winners of	£174,494
1978	3rd	86 winners of	£260,949

Eight Flat-Racing Stables

BIG RACES
The races worth £4,000 or more to the winner were:

1971

HORRIS HILL	Newbury	Disguise	£5,512

1972

GREAT VOLTIGEUR	York	Our Mirage	4,191

1973

JOCKEY CLUB STAKES	Newmarket	Our Mirage	4,335
CHESTER VASE	Chester	Proverb	4,147
HARDWICKE STAKES	Royal Ascot	Rheingold	11,843
JULY STAKES	Newmarket	Dragonara Palace	7,860
RICHMOND STAKES	Goodwood	Dragonara Palace	8,750
ROYAL LODGE	Ascot	Straight as a Die	5,789
JOHN PORTER	Newbury	Rheingold	4,380

1974

JOE CORAL VICTORIA CUP	Ascot	Galiano	4,452
GOODWOOD CUP	Goodwood	Proverb	5,132
YORKSHIRE OAKS	York	Dibidale	13,872
DONCASTER CUP	Doncaster	Proverb	4,881

1975

RICHMOND	Goodwood	Stand to Reason	13,858
GOLD TROPHY	Redcar	Marco Ricci	5,192
EXTEL	Goodwood	Duboff	8,871
SUN CHARIOT	Newmarket	Duboff	8,117

1976

ROSE OF LANCASTER	Haydock	Durtal	4,462
CHILD STAKES	Newmarket	Duboff	6,318
FIRTH OF CLYDE	Ayr	Mofida	4,010
WM HILL CHEVELEY PARK	Newmarket	Durtal	34,426

1977

FRED DARLING	Newbury	Durtal	5,271
PRINCESS ELIZABETH	Epsom	Lady Mere	5,933
SILVER JUBILEE	Kempton	Lord Helpus	7,733
WM HILL TROPHY	York	Mofida	7,140
COCK OF THE NORTH	Haydock	Delta Sierra	6,163
SPORTING CHRONICLE H'CAP	Haydock	Mofida	4,097
ROSE OF LANCASTER	Haydock	Montelimar	6,502
PRINCESS OF WALES	Newmarket	Lord Helpus	12,438
ASCOT STAKES	Royal Ascot	Matinale	4,947
JUBILEE YEAR	Newbury	Delta Sierra	4,791
SEATON DELAVAL	Newcastle	Sexton Blake	8,980

PRINCESS ROYAL	Ascot	Aloft	£7,401
LAURENT PERRIER CHAMPAGNE	Doncaster	Sexton Blake	13,810
1978			
ONE THOUSAND GUINEAS	Newmarket	Enstone Spark	41,130
MUSIDORA	York	Princess of Man	10,264
FEN DITTON	Newmarket	Philodantes	5,026
GORDON	Goodwood	Sexton Blake	11,168
GATWICK HANDICAP	Lingfield	Arapahos	5,560
BENSON AND HEDGES GOLD CUP	York	Hawaiian Sound	49,200
ACOMB	York	Senorita Paquito	4,552
GILBEY CHAMPION TWO-Y-O	York	Two of Diamonds	4,597
PROGRESS NURSERY	Doncaster	Top of the Charts	4,214

BEST RACECOURSES

Haydock Park	40	wins
Pontefract	37	,,
York	37	,,
Newmarket	36	,,
Chester	30	,,
Warwick	28	,,
Newcastle	23	,,
Redcar	22	,,
Bath	21	,,
Kempton	21	,,

JOCKEYS

Ernie Johnson	198	wins	
Willie Carson	106	,,	(former stable jockey, 1 win 1978)
Robert Street	42	,,	
Lester Piggott	41	,,	
Eddie Hide	40	,,	
J. Lynch	13	,,	
Frank Durr	13	,,	
Ray Cochrane	13	,,	
Brian Taylor	7	,,	
Susan Hogan	5	,,	
Paul D'Arcy	5	,,	

His son John won three amateur races in 1978. Suzanne Kane won one, making four in all. Fred Winter won the unique trainers' race at the Kempton Park Centenary meeting on a Hills trained horse. Lord Suffolk and Nick Henderson have won races for him.

BEST MONTHS

July	132 wins
August	101 ,,
June	95 ,,

Hills starts the season earlier than most big trainers.

MULTIPLE WINS

Barry Hills had a six-timer on Saturday, 15th July 1978, comprising Nottingham, Chester (2), Newbury and York (2) with Maryoma, Top of the Charts, Arapahos, Tap On Wood, Yes Please and Miss Zadig. He had a four-timer at Catterick, Epsom and Warwick (2) on 9th June 1978, making 3 four-timers during his career. He has had 10 trebles, one of them in 1978. Also 60 doubles. Most of his doubles and trebles involve more than one course. He selects races very carefully.

OWNERS

He has had approximately 125 winning owners of which some of the most successful have been: Robert Sangster, Charles St George, Henry Zeisel, Jack Stallard, Kalifa Sasi, Mrs P. Pearce (grandmother of Suzanne Kane) and R. Bonnycastle, owner of Enstone Spark.

FIRST WINNERS TRAINED

Flat: La Dolce Vita, Thirsk. Owned B. Dawson, ridden by Ernie Johnson, on 18th April 1969.

RACES FARMED

These include:

RIPON ROWELS	1973, 1975, 1976
DEE STAKES, Chester	1970, 1972, 1973, 1975

NEW COURSE

He had his first winner at Edinburgh with Reine du Soleil on 6th June 1978.

TWO-YEAR-OLD WINNERS

His first two-year-old winner in 1978 was his earliest ever, Sabir at Warwick on 28th March.

GENERAL

Barry Hills sends his horses all over Britain and can be said to have a wider spread than any other trainer. His experience as a travelling head lad has given him 'know how' of all courses. He has also had a considerable number of valuable wins overseas, headed by Rheingold in the Arc in '73 and Dibidale in the Irish Guineas and Oaks in '74.

138

Jeremy Hindley

of Clarehaven, Newmarket

Jeremy Hindley is the son of the late Reg Hindley, Master of Hounds and one of the finest judges of a horse in his day. He was captain of the British Eventing team in the 1952 Olympics. His pack of Harriers, which he hunted for thirty-five years, gave wonderful sport to thousands of Yorkshire men and women.

It was into this sporting and equine atmosphere that Jeremy was born. Inevitably the environment influenced his life—but not as planned.

'It was assumed that when I left Winchester I would work on stud farms and then take on the family stud. That is the Ribblesdale Stud, which was at Gisburn where we lived, but is now at Kirby Moorside,' Jeremy told me as we sat in his long study on the top floor of an old barn at Kremlin House Stables, from where he moved in 1978 to Clarehaven, an historic Newmarket establishment at the end of the Bury Road, where it leads across the Heath towards the Limekilns.

So when Jeremy left school he did the usual round, working with veterinary surgeons and on stud farms. Although he had ridden ponies as a small boy he was not an enthusiastic horseman as a teenager. In fact at one stage he gave up riding. He explained to me that leaving school was virtually tantamount to leaving home, for he soon went to the stud owned by Madame Couturié, near Le Mans, in France. 'She is a wonderful woman,' enthused Jeremy. 'A tremendous character. What she has done for many young Englishmen is beyond praise. She has sorted many of us out. Not only myself but Henry Cecil, Arthur Boyd-Rochfort,

Mikey McCalmont and several others. Well, I did a season there
and followed that with a season with that superb French vet
Edouard Pouret, at his practice near Argentan in Normandy.'

M. Pouret is a friend of Jeremy's. He became a partner with
the trainer and Lady Brigid Ness in Sin Timon, the 1977
Cambridgeshire winner, about which there is an unusual story
later in this chapter. Jeremy also worked under one of the world's
top stud masters, the late Cyril Hall, at the Aga Khan's studs
Ballymany, Sheshoon, Gilltown and Williamstown in Ireland.

'I suppose a fair amount of their teaching rubbed off on me, and
I am most grateful for all they did to help, but the fact is that
having worked on these places I reckoned that stud farming was a
little bit slow for me. I realised that I was more keen on the racecourse than the stud farm,' Jeremy revealed to me and, in so doing,
fell into line with Henry Cecil.

It was during this period when his ambitions were crystallising
that his enthusiasm for riding was rekindled. When he was twenty
Jeremy went to see Bertie Hill, an Olympic team mate of his
father's. He asked Bertie if he would brush up his skill in the
saddle. He wanted to ride in point-to-points and amateur riders'
races under Jockey Club and National Hunt rules. Hill put him right
and so Jeremy set foot on the path which led him to the thrills,
spills, successes and disappointments of the racecourse.

He bought some old selling steeplechasers and started riding
in a few point-to-points. He was lucky enough to be able to take
his horses to Lambourn where he based himself and his small
string with Tim Forster, the talented and consistently successful
trainer of National Hunt winners which include Well To Do, 1972
winner of the Grand National, bought for only £750 in 1966 by
the late Heather Sumner.

Somehow when he was at Lambourn he managed to work for a
year at Cirencester Agricultural College. 'Maybe we ought to
put it the other way round!' cracked Jeremy. 'To be frank I was
messing around a bit, it was all great fun and undoubtedly I learnt
a lot.' Eventually it was time to move on and he left Lambourn
with his horses. He was twenty-three and burning to get on with
the job—to go places. In his mind there was only one place to be
—Newmarket. There he went taking a couple of 'chasers with

him. He wanted to find a trainer who didn't have an assistant, but who could do with one. After some frustrations he found a vacancy with Harry Thomson Jones (better known as Tom Jones). 'Really I think this was the best stroke of luck in my career,' confided Jeremy to me. 'Tom was a great friend and supporter as indeed he has been and will probably continue to be to a great many young people, beginners at the training game. Tom was tremendously encouraging. I worked around the yard, helped the head lad and did other chores. I was lucky enough to ride about twenty winners over jumps.'

Jeremy also had the priceless experience of a year at Warren Place with Sir Noel Murless, one of the world's great horse-masters.

Although he learned, as he puts it, 'quite a bit' with Noel, Jeremy insists 'I always say, and mean it, that my greatest supporter as far as the training side goes was Tom Jones'. Jeremy cited another instance of Tom's help to a budding trainer: he took on Michael Stout, now doing so well at Newmarket.

After his year at Warren Place Jeremy had no intention of starting training immediately. Stables were chock-a-block and it was hard to get a yard at that time (1971).

Jeremy insists that his career has been made easier by the fact that he has never been 'really short of a penny', and that he has (like John Dunlop) been at the right place at the right time. As it happened, hardly had Jeremy left Warren Place when Teddy Lambton announced that he was giving up training and that Kremlin House was for sale. Jeremy has always been able to make snap decisions. He made one then. 'I bought it overnight. It was rather run down. But I had a yard, and although I had not intended to start training so soon, and in any case it was too late to start that year, I had plenty of time to get things organised. So Sally, my wife—we married in 1968—and I were able to spend several months getting things as we wanted them and to think about finding senior staff. I looked round for lads and got ready.'

Jeremy has since added lustre to the racing history of Kremlin House which was built by Prince Demitri Soltykoff, a Russian who came to England in 1856 and stayed until he died in 1903. Tom

141

Jeremy Hindley with his head lad Bill Henderson.

Jennings, senior, my great grandfather, trained the Prince's Sheen to win the Cesarewitch, and Gold to win the Ascot Gold Cup in 1890.

Kremlin House was built in 1874 and the first trainer there was Tom Fordham. Charlie Waugh followed him. He was succeeded by T. Hammond. Other names connected with these stables are

Joe Butters, father of Frank and Fred both of whom trained Derby winners. Joe was at Kremlin House in 1904. The nearest he came to winning a Classic was with Nassovian who was beaten a neck and a head by Fiffinella and Kwang-su in the wartime substitute Derby of 1916. The Hon. George Lambton and Frank Barling also trained at Kremlin.

Jeremy's first win as a trainer there was with Hardship ridden by Brough Scott, in a two-mile novice hurdle at Warwick on Tuesday, 8th December 1970. In the words of Maurice Chevalier, in one of his delightful songs, Jeremy echoed 'Yes, I remember it well. Brough rode superbly a horse that was, to say the least, a difficult customer.' Jeremy then paid another tribute to Brough, who was also based with Tim Forster: 'Brough was ahead of me in the racing game and was a great adviser to me on the National Hunt scene.'

Jeremy had half a dozen winners that first year, mainly 'the old crabs' he had been riding before he took out his trainer's licence. These winners served the very useful purpose of 'getting the show on the road', as Jeremy put it. Then he followed with some remarks which are an accurate and succinct summing up of his professional beginnings: 'Well, I had made a start. I'd been knocking around. I had assimilated things by doing just that. I don't think I had ever worked particularly hard or been of much help to anybody. I don't think I've had as tough a struggle as anybody else. For one thing I've been in reasonable financial shape. I didn't have any owners of course. They all had to be found.

'We have just gone on step by step improving since 1970. I wouldn't say we have been outstandingly lucky. Not lucky, that is, in the way of having several tip-top horses although we have had some good ones. We have not had a classic horse yet, but we have for several years featured in the top twelve in the trainer's list when taking into account winnings abroad as well as those at home.'

Jeremy considers that he has been very lucky with his staff. Bill Henderson, his top-class head man, was travelling head man with Tom Jones for many years. Bill was tired of the travelling and wanted to be more at home. So it fitted in with Jeremy's plans admirably.

'I've still got several lads who started with me and they form the nucleus of my team,' said Jeremy. 'We have our difficulties of course—there isn't a stable that does not, but we get on very well on the whole.'

Jeremy is aided by Tony Esler, who is really a personal assistant in the matter of running the office and all the business connected with an eight-strong team of horses. He has ridden winners here and in Ireland where he was secretary to Paddy Sleator in Co. Wicklow.

Tony Kimberley is another loyal and much appreciated member of the Hindley team. He joined the stable as a lad having been apprenticed to Sir Gordon Richards. Gordon retired the year Jeremy started, so Tony was in luck. The terms of his employment with Jeremy were that he should get a lad's wages with the promise of twenty rides in public or the cash equivalent. Tony has done very well as stable jockey and is, in Jeremy's opinion, extremely under-rated. He began to be successful at a comparatively late stage in his career. He is marvellous on two-year-olds, an accurate judge of pace, and a wise judge after a race, by which I mean that not only can he tell you plenty about the horse he has ridden but he can fill you in on how some of the others went as well. He is fairly strong in the saddle. 'I suppose he might just get beaten a neck by the top three or four in a desperate finish. They can't all be Lester Piggotts. Tony is a bit of a success story,' enthused Jeremy.

Alfred Anthony Kimberley rode one of the greatest races of his life, according to his boss, when he won the Geoffrey Freer Stakes, a £12,440 Group 2 race, at Newbury in 1976, on Swell Fellow. He made all the running and was able to keep just enough in hand to hold off Oats, third to Empery and Relkino in the Derby, and ridden by Pat Eddery.

'Tony has ridden some wonderful races,' insisted Jeremy. 'He often emulates the confidence of Lester Piggott. I suppose one can say that he really has no right to show such assurance but I think it pays off. I am sure Tony has ridden some extraordinary good races without receiving the recognition due to him.'

144

*　　　*　　　*

As an observer of the racing scene and as one who has enjoyed the challenge of daily tipping of horses in a newspaper and on television, I have noticed that Jeremy's two-year-olds are not raced very much in the first part of the season unless of course his stable harbours a precocious youngster. I challenged him on this and he replied: 'I don't hurry my two-year-olds. As a matter of fact I don't like training two-year-olds very much, and also I don't like running them unless they really need to be raced. However, don't forget that I won eight races with The Go-Between, six with Hand Canter and six with Giriama. For me the fun to be had is training three-year-olds and older horses, preferably over a distance of ground. Even several of those people I am lucky enough to train for say repeatedly there is no urgency, but actually when it comes down to it they are in more of a hurry than they make out. One has to remember that there is also a new type of owner, notably gentlemen from the Middle East.'

Jeremy pointed out that if this type of man buys a horse for a lot of money it is imperative for the trainer to keep him interested in his animal: 'He wants to see it run, however much it may be explained to him that the whole thing does take time. Trainers have to adapt themselves more than ever to the requirements of the people who pay the bills. This often goes against trainers' inclinations, and I think it does so with me,' he admitted.

'Another point I would like to make is that when you start training from an empty stable, basically your owners are going to be new to the game. They are going to be owners you have found yourself, or through an agent. They are not generally the old school of owners who understand the game. I don't have any very strong views about training and placing horses except that Newmarket is the best centre in which to train. Sometimes it is criticised by outsiders, I think it always has been, but here you have everything in the way of gallops and facilities.

'What is interesting is that I find that we have to gallop our horses at Newmarket rather more than at many other centres including establishments on downland. Newmarket is comparatively flat and the Heath is light land, whereas downland and many other training gallops are often much stiffer and take more out of a horse. Here at Newmarket this may result in a fraction more wastage from the soundness point of view. This is a criticism that I think is outweighed by the fact that you know more about your horses. You can therefore be more accurate when you place them.

'I think one of the most relevant statistics about training which has only been produced in recent years is the percentage of winners to runners. In 1976 seven out of the first ten trainers in that statistic were Newmarket-based.'

His personal view about placing horses is that of one of the Turf's most powerful rulers and administrators, Admiral Rous, which is to the effect that a trainer and owner should keep themselves in the best company and their horses in the worst.

The Jeremy Hindley-trained Crash Course just failing to hold off Sagaro (Lester Piggott) in the 1976 Ascot Gold Cup. (Sport & General)

He does not mind where he sends a horse. He said with some vehemence 'If a horse is a Hamilton horse then he has got to go to Hamilton if he has to win a race. No point in running him at Sandown where he would be outclassed.'

His belief, now widely accepted among trainers, is that the motorways facilitate the placing of horses at distant racecourses. This I might add is not only the perquisite of the powerful Southern stables, but acts increasingly in reverse with more North Country runners at the southern meetings and is well exploited by such men as Bill Elsey, Gordon Richards, Bill Watts and the Easterby brothers.

Another of Jeremy's views is that although Newmarket is not near any racecourse except its own, it is not too far from many others. There may not be a flat meeting within sixty miles of Newmarket but thanks to the new roads horses are not prohibited from going anywhere in a few hours.

Changing the subject I asked Jeremy which horses had given him the most pleasure to train. His reply was that most of his horses had given him a lot of fun. There were two which had given him outstanding pleasure because they had looked as if they would not stand training but had survived to win good races. They were Crash Course and Street Light.

'Crash Course was a very high class stayer,' related Jeremy. 'He was not a sound horse as a four- and five-year-old. He was only beaten a length by Sagaro in the 1976 Ascot Gold Cup. In fact Crash Course was lame during Royal Ascot week. He was lame three days before the race, two days before the race and the day before the race! Each day he had been gradually less lame and on the morning of the race he was just about sound. He put up a marvellous performance. Sagaro won the Gold Cup in 1975, 1976 and 1977 but none of the horses he beat got as close to him as Crash Course.

'He would have given Sagaro a tremendous race if he had not had that setback,' said Jeremy and then as if to give his words extra emphasis lit his pipe with a ferocious click of his lighter.

Crash Course was an unlucky horse. Not only did he have hock trouble but tendon problems as well. He fell in the 1975 Goodwood

A major Handicap triumph for Jeremy Hindley—Sin Timon ridden by Tony Kimberley wins the 1977 Irish Sweeps Cambridgeshire at Newmarket. (Sport & General)

Cup when he was favourite and more or less a certainty.

The toughest animal ever trained by Jeremy at Kremlin House was the filly Street Light. She had a serious lameness in each of her racing seasons.

Each lameness looked as though it would be curtains for her, but she came back every time and won a good race. She also collected a Group 3 race at Deauville, the Prix de Meautry. She was fantastically tough to have done that because usually sprinters, once they have 'gone', tend to have folded up for good. One must

148

remember that the margins in merit among the top sprinters are small.

'She was only tiny and had comparatively little bone,' Jeremy added. 'Not surprisingly I was very fond of her.'

I think that the story of Sin Timon's inclusion as a member of the Kremlin House and subsequently based Clarehaven team is, to say the least, unusual. His trainer bought him at Doncaster Sales as a yearling for only 4,400 guineas. He is by Captain's Gig, sire of good winners, out of Ilsebill by Birkhahn, a mare with a top class European pedigree. She is a half-sister to two German classic winners.

'Why we bought him so cheaply,' Jeremy told me, 'was that Sin Timon was in considerable pain at the sales. He had a tail bandage put on very tightly presumably on the way over from the stud of his breeder Princess A. Oettingen-Spielberg.'

This tight bandage had more or less killed the circulation in the tail so the colt looked fairly unprepossessing. When Sin Timon arrived at Kremlin House his tail effectively fell off. All the hair came out and for some days the tail bone looked dead. Jeremy was apprehensive that some of this bone would fall off too.

'So,' related Sin Timon's part owner and trainer, 'I had a tail-less horse with a very smelly stump to what was left! He was not particularly easy to sell. But anyway Edouard Pouret was in England and as he had had several mares from the same female line and knew the breed, he took a third share and Lady Brigid Ness bought the remaining third. They called him Sin Timon which is Spanish for 'without a rudder'.

Little by little the tail grew again. The rest of Sin Timon was also slow to develop and he took a long time 'to come to anything'. In his trainer's opinion the colt has always been a Pattern race horse. 'He was just about a "half decent" horse in 1977 when he won the Cambridgeshire as a three-year-old with eight stone three pounds.'

He was really not right for most of the summer of 1977. He had some moderate form and some fairly lengthy absences from the racecourse. Only in the autumn did he come back to something like his real self.

Jeremy has been in the game long enough now to appreciate the loyalty of several owners. 'I have been lucky to them as well,' Jeremy reminded me. 'In particular there is Mrs Muriel Haggas and her son Brian. Actually my first yearling order was for him, but I have been luckier on the racecourse for his mother. They are the sort of people one really enjoys training for. Then there is Jimmy Crichton-Stuart. He owns Swell Fellow, a winner of more than £40,000. Quite a good score for a gelding.'

Another owner who has been most helpful and lucky for Jeremy is Lord Harrington, who incidentally was so successful in choosing yearlings for Mr David Robinson when his several stables (including Clarehaven) were winning dozens of races each season. Bill Harrington bred and owned Street Light.

When I quizzed Jeremy about the good horses he has trained he said with conviction, 'I only count as good horses those with which I have managed to win a Pattern race.' (The Pattern race scheme provides a comprehensive series of tests for the best horses of various ages.) 'The Pattern race scheme,' Jeremy went on, 'is the basis for good horses. The best horse we have had here so far is probably He Loves Me. He just about heads the list I would think, but Crash Course comes very near him.'

He Loves Me won the Hungerford Stakes at Newbury in August 1977. He beat the older horses Radetzky and Boldboy decisively in this seven furlong event. The reason why his trainer was diffident about putting He Loves Me in front of Crash Course is that they both raced over very different distances. 'Don't forget,' he said, 'Crash Course was a really good stayer. He had a lot of bad luck. It is not easy to compare them.'

The Pattern race winners the stable has had are He Loves Me, Street Light, Crash Course, Be Tuneful, Swell Fellow, The Go-Between, Northern Princess, Blessed Rock, Some Hand and Persian Market, who didn't really win a Pattern race but was handed one as a result of a disqualification.

The trainer's view on handicaps is, 'I don't reckon to be a handicap specialist. The first time one of my horses sets foot on a racecourse he is doing his best from that moment onwards. I would not pretend to be any good at laying out a horse for a handicap. If they win a good handicap on the way up the chances

150

are they are going to win Pattern races eventually. Of course we have won some good handicaps along the line, such as the Cambridgeshire, the City and Suburban, two Joe Coral Autumn Cups, two Ascot Stakes, two William Hill Gold Trophies, run over six furlongs at York's June meeting, a Bovis Handicap and an Ayrshire Handicap. With the exception of Coed Cochion and Sin Timon all my horses which have won decent races have won Pattern races.'

A very noteworthy contribution which Jeremy has made to Turf reform concerns Limited Handicaps. As most of us are aware there can be a range of 35 lb between the top and bottom weights in a handicap race. In the opinion of Jeremy and others there was a

Rated by Jeremy Hindley as one of the best horses he has trained, He Loves Me (Joe Mercer), wins the Cork and Orrery Stakes at Royal Ascot, 1977. (Sport & General)

desperate need for some handicaps with a smaller weight range.

Let Jeremy tell us in his own words why he wrote a paper for the Trainers' Federation of which he is a Council member, for the eventual consideration of the Jockey Club: 'The need for limited handicaps was based on the fact that we have quite a weak structure of Condition races. There are not many of them. There are also the Pattern races. Below that level there are very few non-handicap races for what I can best call the nearly-good horse. I think this horse gets a raw deal in England.

'As a trainer you buy a horse of this type for an owner. You don't do so badly because the horse proves above average. He wins a maiden race or two, then takes a couple of handicaps but he is not quite good enough for Pattern races. There are then very few places you can go with that horse unless you run him in handicaps in which he will get top weight and have too much to do. Therefore the best possible thing you can do for your owner is to advise him to sell the horse abroad to race. He may be sold for quite a good price but really this is the kind of horse which should be encouraged to stay at home but if he does and then wins a handicap he will be asked to give 35 lb to some horses in the future. That's too much to give away particularly if something down the bottom of the weights has been "on the fiddle".'

Jeremy's final point is that if there are limited handicaps with a weight range of 14 lb or 21 lb at most then not only does the good horse have a chance but the 'nearly-good' one as well.

The Jockey Club introduced Limited Handicaps in 1977. Jeremy was particularly pleased to see that the first race of this type which was run at Newmarket—the Fen Ditton Handicap (1 m) on 16th July—attracted a classic winner, Mrs McArdy. She won the Fen Ditton Handicap with 9 st 7 lb. The Jockey Club was encouraged by the success of this type of race and more have been introduced.

It could of course be said that this type of race is not really meant for classic winners. The answer to this is that only rarely will a classic winner be found in a Limited Handicap. To begin with there are very few classic winners about and the Mrs McArdys of the Turf are usually otherwise engaged.

*   *   *

It was in the late summer of 1977 that Jeremy made the interesting announcement (an exclusive by the *Sporting Life*'s Newmarket correspondent Tony Jacobson) that he has purchased Clarehaven. This was built by Peter Purcell Gilpin out of his winnings from a four-year-old filly, Clarehaven, trained by him to win the Cesarewitch in 1900. It was in 1903 that Clarehaven sheltered that superb racehorse, then a two-year-old, Major Eustace Loder's Pretty Polly, who became the first of several classic winners to be trained there.

Other trainers who have been successful at Clarehaven include Geoffrey Brooke, who was a wonderful handler of two-year-olds including Our Babu, winner of the 1955 Two Thousand Guineas, Ryan Jarvis, now at Phantom House, and Paul Davey who was a private trainer to Mr David Robinson, and who gave him a superb beginning to his tremendous venture as an owner on an almost unprecedented scale when he won with Floretty, Little Green Man, Carlburg, London Boy and River Peace on Easter Saturday, 1968. Yellow God was perhaps the greatest sprinter trained for Mr Robinson by Paul Davey and it is gratifying that this horse has made his mark as a stallion.

My colleague Richard Onslow says in his admirable book *The Heath and the Turf* published by Arthur Barker in 1971 : 'The big house at Clarehaven which Peter Purcell Gilpin had built and Sir Alfred Butt had lived in while the Clarehaven trainers had had a smaller house nearer the yard, Mr Robinson demolished, replacing it with a luxurious modern residence.' It is to this lovely house and accompanying stables that the enthusiastic and dedicated trainer Jeremy Hindley with his charming wife Sally, his three young daughters, Rebecca, Victoria and Martha, his devoted staff and powerful team of seventy horses have moved.

Jeremy hoped that 1978, his first season based on Clarehaven, would be a good one. He appeared to have some useful horses full of potential but that is not how things went. 'We had rather a quiet year. No excuses. The horses were very well and settled marvellously into their new quarters. The trouble was that on the whole the horses were not much good,' he told me.

When I last spoke to Jeremy in connection with this book he

had sent out around forty winners and was hoping to have a few more by the close. He classified this total as 'barely respectable' but by any standard he can be said to have done reasonably well. However he is a man who aims high and is unlikely to lower his sights.

Meistersinger, winner of the Moreland Brewery Trophy at Newbury is, Jeremy believes, really a horse for 1979, meaning that he should improve. Sin Timon, his 1977 Cambridgeshire winner, won a good handicap at York and subsequently broke down.

Warmington, a colt by Homeguard out of a mare by Floribunda, was, in the autumn of 1978, the stable's chief hope for the 1979 top class three-year-old races. He beat Tap on Wood at Ayr in August and Golden River at Newmarket over seven furlongs at the end of the month. 'Warmington may not stay well enough to be a Derby colt but he should certainly be good enough for Pattern races. Like Meistersinger I think he will be a relatively better horse in 1979 than he was as a two-year-old,' Jeremy said. Shortly after this prophecy the colt was placed in the Dewhurst Stakes and in the William Hill Futurity.

Followers of the Clarehaven string will be interested to know that Jeremy's policy for 1979 and probably in subsequent years will be to restrict the number of horses in his stable to sixty-five. 'I find,' he told me, 'that I have enough efficient staff—the nucleus which stays put—to run a string that size.'

Times change and so do policies. In future, whether Jeremy has a bigger team, a smaller one or keeps the figure at around sixty-five, I am as certain as I can be that his horses will always be well cherished and trained, and we can expect Clarehaven to enjoy a renewal of its illustrious days.

A charming Hindley family group: Sally and Jeremy with their three daughters (left to right) Rebecca (holding 'Dickie Davies'), Martha, and Victoria with 'Sailor'. (Brian Love)

STATISTICAL RECORDS

Jeremy Hindley has had 8 complete seasons on the Flat and 283 wins of £427,116 in Britain under Jockey Club rules. He won 98 races worth more than £1,000 between 1971 and 1977 inclusive and eight races worth more than £2,000 to the winner in 1978. He has won Pattern races in France and Scandinavia.

BIG RACES
The races worth £4,000 or more to the winner were:

1972

WM HILL MEM GOLD CUP	York	Some Hand	£4,951

1974

RIBBLESDALE STAKES	Royal Ascot	Northern Princess	10,097
AYRSHIRE HANDICAP	Ayr	Swell Fellow	5,135
BOVIS HANDICAP	Ascot	Street Light	4,191

1975

GLENLIVET HANDICAP	Newmarket	Be Tuneful	4,055
MIDDAY SUN STAKES	Lingfield	Tudor Crown	6,367
WM HILL GOLD TROPHY	York	Be Tuneful	4,603
DONCASTER CUP	Doncaster	Crash Course	4,829
JOE CORAL AUTUMN CUP	Newbury	Coed Cochion	6,201
CHALLENGE STAKES	Newmarket	Be Tuneful	4,676

1976

ASCOT STAKES	Royal Ascot	Tudor Crown	4,667
QUEEN ALEXANDRA STAKES	Royal Ascot	Coed Cochion	4,091
HARRY PEACOCK STAKES	Newcastle	Game Lord	4,063
GEOFFREY FREER STAKES	Newbury	Swell Fellow	12,400

1977

CLERICAL MEDICAL GREENHAM	Newbury	He Loves Me	9,455
CORK AND ORRERY	Royal Ascot	He Loves Me	8,571
HUNGERFORD	Newbury	He Loves Me	8,374
NORTHERN GOLDSMITHS	Newcastle	Sin Timon	6,258
JOE CORAL AUTUMN CUP	Newbury	Nearly A Hand	7,546
IRISH SWEEPS CAMBRIDGESHIRE	Newmarket	Sin Timon	10,817

1978

HAMBLETON STAKES	York	Sin Timon	7,139
SANDLEFORD	Newbury	Double Lock	3,298
H T S AIR CHARTER	Newmarket	Nonchalant	3,476
DURHAM	Newcastle	Moon Sammy	4,073
MORLAND BREWERY	Newbury	Meistersinger	5,202

| HERONSLEA | Ayr | Warmington | £4,539 |
| FITZROY HOUSE | Newmarket | Warmington | 4,266 |

Big races won more than once :
    William Hill Gold Cup ('72 and '75)
    Lupe Stakes, Goodwood ('74 and '75)
    Ascot Stakes, Royal Ascot ('75 and '76)
He has also won the Prix de Meautry at Deauville twice.

BEST RACECOURSES

Newmarket	35 wins
Yarmouth	32 ,,
Ayr	16 ,,
Beverley	14 ,,
York	14 ,,
Ascot	13 ,,
Newbury	13 ,,
Doncaster	11 ,,
Ripon	10 ,,
Nottingham	10 ,,

JOCKEYS

A. Kimberley began to ride winners for Hindley in his second season as a trainer and is stable jockey.

A. Kimberley	162 wins
L. Piggott	28 ,,
N. Crowther	21 ,,
J. Mercer	18 ,,

BEST MONTHS

July	59 wins
August	55 ,,
June	48 ,,
May	35 ,,

He has not had a March winner and only two November winners.

MULTIPLE WINS

He has had 29 doubles, three trebles. Four doubles at Yarmouth, three at Newmarket.

OWNERS

A considerable proportion of winners have been owned by himself, his wife or members of the Hindley family—they account for approximately 50 wins. Mrs Muriel Haggas and the Haggas family, Mrs D. Heimann and Lord James Crichton Stuart have been markedly successful among his owners, who tend to support him loyally through the years.

157

FIRST WINNERS TRAINED

Jumping: Hardship, Warwick, novice hurdle 2 m. Ridden by Brough Scott. Tuesday, 8th December 1970.

Flat: Fivepenny Piece, Yarmouth, three-year-old maidens at starting. Owned by himself. Ridden by Paul Tulk.

HORSES

Horses which have won in several seasons for him: Some Hand ('71, '72, '73), Tudor Crown ('74, '75, '76) and Coed Cochion ('74, '75, '76).

Bruce Hobbs

of Palace House, Newmarket

Bruce Hobbs was seventeen years old when he rode Battleship to win the Grand National in 1938. He was the youngest rider to win this famous steeplechase and Battleship possibly the smallest horse to do so.

When Lester Piggott rode his first winner at Haydock at the age of fourteen I remember my father, Eric, who was there, telling me that Keith Piggott's boy might make as fine a jockey as Fred Archer and he would outshine his father who had ridden extremely well over hurdles and fences.

Some years before Piggott's first winner my father saw Bruce win at Aintree and although that was not the lad's first win over fences by any means the feeling was that, apart from the kudos of winning the National, the son of Reg would make an even greater name for himself than his father, once a good rider and then a top N.H. trainer. Whereas Lester went flying ahead in spite of one or two temporary checks, Bruce's ambition to become the best National Hunt rider was thwarted by three outstanding occurrences. He broke his back. He went off to fight for his country in World War II. When he came home after four years he had grown too heavy to resume a career as a successful jump jockey.

Some of the trainers I have written about in this book reached important positions comparatively quickly but Bruce has had to struggle and it is only in the last few years, when in middle age, that he has emerged head and shoulders above all but a very few of his rivals. In other words, he 'made it', much to the joy of his father, who after a distinguished career with horses, died in 1978.

Back in 1939, Bruce Hobbs with his father Reg outside the weighing room at the Cheltenham National Hunt Festival. (Gloucestershire Echo)

*   *   *

Let us go back to his beginnings as Bruce told me about them one evening at Palace House Stables, Newmarket, possibly the most historic training establishment site in the country and certainly the oldest in Newmarket. Some of the stables in that yard were there in the days of the Stuarts and there cannot be much doubt that Royal horses used them.

'Father was Master of the Horse in America for twenty-three years for Mr Ambrose Clark who loved horses, hunting and racing,' Bruce told me. 'I was born there and when we came back to England in 1921 we lived at Melton Mowbray in the heart of the hunting shires, so loved by Americans even today. Father managed fifty thoroughbred hunters for Ambrose Clark and his family, who came from Long Island.

160

'I began riding when I was four. I hunted with the Quorn when I was six. I had a very good show pony called Lady Marvel, who started her working life in a fishmonger's cart in Leicester. She won more than a hundred first prizes for me both showing and show jumping. I hunted, when I was away from school, a couple of times a week. My father was at it six days a week. He also rode in point-to-points and hunter 'chases, and retained a few.'

In the early Thirties the Ambrose Clark family decided to close down the big hunting enterprise at Melton Mowbray. Reg Hobbs had by then got the training bug. His friend Harry Cottrill, who trained for Sir Abe Bailey and was father of Humphrey, also for some years a leading trainer, was at Seven Barrows, Lambourn, where Peter Walwyn trains. Harry found a place for Reg to train in Lambourn. He moved there in 1932 and had a stable of jumpers. Bruce became involved and had his first ride as a fourteen-year-old amateur at Stratford-on-Avon, on Thoughtless II, in a hurdle race.

He rode his first winner on Mrs James de Rothschild's Amida at Wolverhampton in March 1936. Mrs de Rothschild, more than forty years after that great day, is one of his patrons at Palace House Stables.

Bruce did quite well but in those days the son of a licensed trainer could no longer ride as an amateur when he had scored ten winners. Then he had to apply for a permit. As he was the son of a licensed trainer and without any private means he turned professional—on his sixteenth birthday.

'I remember it all very well because I was at Wolverhampton where I had ridden my first winner. My licence was telegraphed through there by Weatherbys. I had my first two rides there as a professional on 28th December, the day after my sixteenth birthday. They both won. They were the hurdlers Baccharis and Eliza.' The same day he rode Mrs Marion Scott's Battleship into second place behind Lady Lindsay's Antipas in the Oteley Chase.

Battleship, an entire horse, standing fifteen hands one and a half inches, could have been the smallest horse to win the National, but that erudite racing scribe of those days, Mankato, asserted that Casse Tête, a mare, was certainly not more than fifteen two. She won in 1872. Four years later Regal was a fifteen two

National hero. Father O'Flynn, 1892, was thought to be smaller than Battleship. Abd-el-cader who won in 1850 and 1851 was about the same height as Battleship.

Smallest horse or not, Battleship was sent over specially to win the National by Mrs Marian Scott, a member of the affluent Dupont family. Mrs Scott was the instigator of the Colonial Cup, a famous steeplechase in America, to which English and Irish owners occasionally send a runner. Battleship was sent to Reg Hobbs in 1936 and Tim Hamey, who won the Grand National on Forbra in 1932, rode Battleship in his first few races in this country before Bruce took over and won several races on the little horse.

Battleship, one of the very few entire horses to win the National, also won the American Grand National and over most distances from four and a half furlongs to four and a half miles. He did not run again after the Aintree Grand National. He returned to America and was successful at stud siring three individual sons to win the American Grand National.

He also sired Stakes winners. He was by Man O' War, one of the great horses of the world, and was out of Quarantine, half sister to Quenouille, winner of the French Oaks (1919), in the Rothschild colours, and third dam of En Fraude, the 1937 French Oaks winner.

'That was the sort of class he was,' enthused Bruce. 'My father always said that had he come over here as a four- or five-year-old he would have won the Ascot Gold Cup.

'I was to ride Mrs Ambrose Clark's Flying Minutes in the 1938 Grand National. I had ridden him in the race in 1937 and fell off, otherwise I think I would have been placed behind Royal Mail. Anyhow he went wrong which left us with three other runners, What Have You, Battleship and Bagatelle. I didn't fancy any of them and to be quite honest, I only rode Battleship because I was offered more to ride him than I was for the other two!

'I won't go on about the National. As you know Battleship managed to catch Royal Danielli, ridden by Dan Moore, a few strides from the post, much to the chagrin of the Irish.

Trooper Bruce Hobbs in 1940, nearly two years after winning the Grand National on Battleship.

'I broke my back in a selling hurdle at Cheltenham in November that year. I was off for six months and forty years later still get terrible pains in my back, but I have learned to live with them.

'The last winner I rode before going off to the war in Palestine was Lord Bicester's Asterabad at Windsor in 1939. He was trained by George Beeby, father of Harry, one of Britain's leading auctioneers of thoroughbreds. Incidentally George asked me to ride that super old chaser Delaneige in the 1938 Grand National. I would have done so had not Fulke Walwyn, the stable jockey who was crocked, been pronounced fit to ride the horse three days before the race.'

I have dwelt at some length on Bruce's earlier days because it reveals some of the trials and the successes which have helped to mould the character of this man, one of the country's great horse-masters.

Bruce was away for four years in the Middle East during the war. He came back in September 1944 with an M.C. and hoped to ride another winner or two before he packed up but he found his weight and wasting more than he could stand.

It was at this difficult time that Bruce, walking back one night from the station after a visit to the Turkish baths, was given a lift by Fulke Walwyn. 'Fulke had just resumed training but had been posted to Germany. He asked me if I would take over the reins while he was abroad. I did. That was a bit of luck and a great experience,' Bruce recalled.

'Eventually I had to find something to do, so I put an advertisement in the *Racing Calendar* for a job as an assistant or private trainer. I had a number of replies. The one I fancied most was from Mr and Mrs John Rogerson. I arranged an interview with them at Newmarket on the day Dante won a wartime Derby there.'

Jack Anthony, one of the trio of Anthony brothers who were fine trainers, was a friend of the Hobbs family and lived at Letcombe Regis. He drove Bruce to Newmarket. There Bruce met Mr and Mrs Rogerson and they gave him the job as their private trainer. They had a few horses in training at Newmarket at that time but no place of their own.

Although Bruce didn't realise it at the time, he had left home for good. After the Derby he went back to Letcombe Regis with Jack. From there he had a good look round for some stables for the Rogersons' horses. He scoured Sussex and will never forget the late Towser Gosden's help. However, he didn't find anything so he went back to Letcombe Regis where he had already met his wife to be, Betty Jean Winder. Bruce told me, 'There was a place available at Letcombe by then. I was having serious walk-out with Betty. So we got engaged and I told the Rogersons.'

The Winders were great friends of Jack and it was actually while staying with Jack Anthony that Bruce met Betty. Like all the trainers I have written about in this book Bruce is deeply indebted to the backing he has had from his wife. He wrote to me once : 'Any success that has come my way Betty must share. We have been together a long time now and have been through some difficult times. No matter what the situation Betty has always been there, encouraging and advising. Most certainly I should never have got anywhere without her.'

The stables Bruce found eventually were practically next door to Jack Anthony at Letcombe Regis. Bruce and Betty were married and he trained for the Rogersons for five years. Probably the best horse he trained there was the grey chaser War Risk, by Cri de Guerre. He won the Grand Sefton Chase at Aintree in 1946.

Bob Turnell, a superb horseman, became first jockey to the stable just after the end of the war. He had been riding since 1928 but he had only just lost his allowance to claim. In those days a jockey had to ride fifteen winners to lose his 5 lb allowance. Bob had obviously been slow to get going, excellent rider though he was. He and Bruce became firm friends and Bruce was delighted with Bob's riding.

At the end of five years as private trainer to John Rogerson Bruce took stock. He was not doing badly but the enterprise was not paying. He went straight to John Rogerson and told him. In a previous review of the situation the Rogersons had given him permission to carry on as a public trainer in an attempt to enable him to make ends meet.

'Anyhow it was no good and John Rogerson was kind and

understanding about it,' Bruce recalled.

Like so many young men who begin in jumping stables Bruce wanted, as he put it, 'to get flat racing'. This he did. That fine trainer of jumpers and flat racers, George Beeby, who died in 1977, gave him a job as assistant.

'It was when that super sprinter Grey Sovereign was a two-year-old that we moved to George's place at Compton,' Bruce said, and admitted that he learned a lot from George who in those days had betting owners and a stable full of sprinters. 'My word, he used to get them tuned up, and when they were expected to win they usually did,' enthused Bruce. 'I've not forgotten also what superb chasers Lord Bicester had with George. Such horses as Roimond, Finnure and Silver Fame.'

At that time Harry Carr, the jockey, had a second retainer with George. Bruce became very friendly with Harry and this led to another job for Bruce. In the autumn of 1952 he was at Windsor for George Beeby when Harry said to him, 'Oh, by the way, Captain Boyd-Rochfort would like to see you'.

'I thought, "What the hell does he want me for?"' Bruce recalled. He was very busy at the time and he asked Harry to tell the Captain that he would be free at such and such a time and could he see him then?

'The long and short of it was that The Captain offered me a job as assistant.' Bruce admitted to me that although he asked The Captain for time to think it over he couldn't get in touch with him quick enough. Eventually he went up to Newmarket, saw round the Freemason Lodge Stables, and took the job.

At first the cottage in which Bruce and his wife were to live wasn't ready so he left Betty behind with their baby girl, Aubrine Elizabeth, at Letcombe Regis. Bruce stayed at the Bedford Lodge Hotel, Newmarket, until his quarters at Freemason Lodge were ready when Betty joined him. There they stayed until the beginning of 1960.

Bruce was with The Captain during a period of considerable success. 'We had some marvellous horses,' he reminded me. 'You see, until then the only good flat horse I had anything to do with was Grey Sovereign. I had seen a lot of "scrubbers"—plating fillies and moderate two-year-olds.

166

'Arriving at Freemason Lodge I had to take charge in a big way. I was not only assistant trainer but a sort of head man and general dog's body. What an eye opener for me! There were fifty potential Grey Sovereigns there. The standard Cecil Boyd-Rochfort expected of his team was very high. He would not tolerate what goes on today and in fact I wonder if he would cope, but I am glad to say he and I hit it off. I found him difficult in some ways and he was most fastidious. I had a tricky job running that yard because we didn't have many seasoned stable lads. In fact he took on a lot of apprentices and more and more girls. I was a sort of sergeant major and had to see that those around me got on with the job.

'The Captain was inclined to be off-hand with the staff except for a few old men who had been with him for years. If I wanted to get through to him about a stable boy I was talking about I used to say, "You know him, Sir, the boy who does so and so." Then he registered.'

It was a great experience for Bruce in that yard with a wonderful trainer, with superb horses. When he first went there Her Majesty the Queen's Aureole was a two-year-old. He was quite one of the best horses Bruce has ever seen.

During the eight years Bruce was with the Captain he had the honour—and the luck—to be connected with the training of eight classic winners. They were three Leger winners—Premonition, Alcide and Meld; one winner of the Derby—Parthia; the Two Thousand Guineas—Pall Mall; the One Thousand Guineas—Meld; and the Oaks—Meld. During this time the stable won an Ascot Gold Cup with Zarathustra, and two Doncaster Cups with Agreement.

Bruce learned many things from Cecil Boyd-Rochfort about training racehorses but above all how to condition them. In this respect Cecil Boyd-Rochfort would take endless time to work his horses. 'Never rush when you are working horses, Hobbs,' he would say. 'Work it all out carefully and when you change your riders round before a piece of work, take your time. Put the proper jockeys on the right horses.'

The Captain would never do any work at all until horses had been out for forty-five minutes. He would send them for a walk.

Bruce and Betty Hobbs in Palace House yard, 1978. (Brian Love)

Then probably for another walk and then for a little trot before anything like fast work was attempted. His stayers would be out for at least two and a quarter hours every day.

'This, of course, was right,' Bruce told me. 'You didn't have to gallop them. You got them muscled up and cleared their pipes by working them gradually. That,' he added with emphasis, 'is one of the main things I learnt from The Captain.

'I was in charge of the feeding. Luckily for me I had taken an interest in this all my life. The Captain had his own ideas on this subject. He used to put in such things as soya bean meal and skimmed milk powder, not full milk powder—he thought that would be a bit too fattening. I have carried on the same things here at Palace House because I know they work.

'While I was with The Captain I learned many of the requirements for training a good horse. I don't know if people realise that training a good horse is very different from training a "scrubber". The good 'un has got to have much more attention.

'I had very little to do, as you might expect, with planning a horse's campaign. In fact I didn't have anything to do with the office side of a horse's management, but because I was very close to The Captain I used to know through instinct or intuition what was coming off.

'The Captain would rarely let his horses go round the Midland meetings. There would be well-bred fillies in the yard that would be moderate according to his standards, but would be good things at Leicester or a similar course but he would say, "It is not worth sending her there, Hobbs. The prize money is not enough. I'll win a worthwhile race with her at a decent course." That was in the 1950s. Sure enough it would come in a thousand pound race at Hurst Park or Kempton or somewhere like that. He set himself a very, very high standard. Only the best was good enough.'

Going to Newmarket was a tremendous challenge for Bruce, but as he said to Betty halfway through the first year, 'If you want to train horses this is the only place to be.'

'Everything is laid on for you,' he emphasised to me. 'There are the most wonderful gallops. The Lambourn gallops—I know them inside out—they don't compare with Newmarket. Neither do the

Didcot gallops, nor the Blewbury gallops. I know them all. Here you also have the sales and wonderful racing. In my opinion this is the place—the only place.

'So we adapted ourselves to Newmarket. We were not very sociable. We could not afford to be. I am one-track-minded and putting work first was the only way we could have dealt with the situation then. Well, it paid off. I am not ashamed to say now that when we came to Newmarket I got the princely sum of a tenner a week, plus a house. The stable boys got seven pounds fifty pence. I went up a little bit and by the time I had finished I was getting a thousand a year. We managed.'

The trouble was that Bruce got very frustrated. He was promised that when Cecil Boyd-Rochfort packed up he would get some horses, but there was no sign of Cecil retiring. He had to do something but he didn't know what the hell to do, he told me.

Bruce poured out his heart to a friend, Colonel Bill Gibson, who asked 'Do you want a change?' Bruce said that he did and was invited to join Colonel Gibson's saddlery business in Newmarket. He and his family moved out from Cecil Boyd-Rochfort's in March 1961 and 'sad to say,' commented Bruce, 'there was a little bit of bad blood. He didn't like my going.

'I took on the saddlery job but it was soon obvious that it wasn't going to suit me. I did it for nine months. I don't regret it at all. I learnt a lot about people and travelling the countryside, I went to almost every training establishment. Some of the things I saw made my hair curl. One day I went to see a trainer who was doing quite well. It was in June and very hot. Flies everywhere. He wanted a special type of boot for a filly. We went into her box. The filly laid her ears back, rushed into a corner, and turned her backside on him. Quite undeterred he walked straight up between her hind legs. How he wasn't killed I don't know. Well, as I told you that job didn't last. I got itchy feet again. We were both unsettled and hated not hearing the clatter of buckets in a yard.

'We were at a Newmarket party one night. Mrs George Lambton was there and she said to Betty that she had heard that I would like to get back into racing again. The upshot of this was that Jack Clayton rang me up and offered me a job. Norman Bertie who had held the licence for Jack was retiring for two reasons. His eyesight was poor; and the Jockey Club had said that a licence holder must also hold the leasehold of a training establishment, and of course Norman did not do that.

'The proposition was that Jack would hold the licence and that I would assist him, do all the organising and supervise the work, but he would be in charge. I joined him in January 1962. He had a reputation for being a difficult man, but I got on with Jack Clayton very well. His training methods were fashioned on those of the late Fred Darling. I think this was understandable for he greatly admired the man and of course Norman Bertie had worked for many years with Fred.

'Jack had a very different feeding system from The Captain's. I didn't approve of it and I told him so. He gave me rein and allowed me to reorganise this and it worked.'

'Midway through my second year with him I saw an advertisement in the Racing Calendar for a private trainer. There was a box number. Betty and I said "Nothing venture, nothing gain", so I answered it. We were surprised to have a telephone call. Would I go and meet Mr David Robinson? As you know he was to spend thousands and thousands of pounds on yearlings and to race in a tremendous style for several years. Well, I got the job with him. As I had a contract with Jack I told him what I had done. He did not hold me to my contract, but I stayed with him for the rest of the year. The only man I took with me—I asked Jack if I could have him—was Brian Lunness who I had previously engaged to work for Jack. He has done well since setting up as a trainer himself. I am delighted. Anyway, he came with me to Robinson's as my travelling head lad. He also broke all the yearlings for me. He was with me for the best part of ten years before he struck out on his own.

'I had two years with Robinson. I knew when I took the job I would only last, at most, three years. I realised it was a tremendous challenge because I had the opportunity to tackle something I had always wanted to do.

'We went to Carlburg, in the Bury Road, where Joe Lawson trained for some years. The place had been absolutely gutted. I had to start from scratch and design my own feed house, my

boiler house—everything. There was not a rack and chain anywhere. There was nothing. The builders had surfaced the yard
and it would have been like an ice-rink. There were also a lot of
sharp corners—just the sort to injure horses. We had to make
those corners round and smooth out a lot of other problems.

'In many ways it was a great experience to work for Mr
Robinson, I learnt an awful lot there on the business side, account-
ing and book work. He was fantastically clever on the business
side. I didn't really understand his language and he certainly did
not understand mine. I don't think he expected to, but I was
supposed to learn to understand his. I am not grumbling. He was
the boss. But for him and being allowed to get among the sort of
horses he had, I don't think we would ever have been in the
position we are now.

'The first winner I trained for him was Ward Drill, ridden by
Harry Carr, in the Blue Peter Stakes at Newmarket. Harry rode
for me when The Captain did not want him. I finished up my first
season with nineteen winners. One was Mrs Robinson's Ruby
Wedding, successful in the Midland Cambridgeshire. But we
were having our troubles even then. The next year we had some
nice horses including Cambridge, Enrico, Wandering Eyes,
London Way, My Heart and Suvretta. We won races, but I am
sorry to say I was not getting on with the boss, and as I had upset
him in some way he said he wanted me to resign. I told him I
wouldn't. So he sacked me. This was the only time I have been
sacked. I left in November 1965 and as far as I was concerned
there was no animosity. The question was where was I going?'

After a lot of thought Betty had a chat with old friends Douglas
and Joan Gray. The Grays made some very helpful suggestions
which in time resulted in Mr Jim Phillips, Mr Tom Blackwell,
Mr Jocelyn Hambro and Mr David Wills coming to Bruce's aid.
They formed a company with Bruce as trainer. After much
discussion they took a lease on Palace House Stables. Since those
days Jim Phillips has retired from the board. Tom Blackwell
became chairman and Bruce has joined the board.

Bruce and Betty Hobbs moved into Palace House on 7th
February 1966, two days after his father's birthday and the wedding

day of his daughter Aubrine Elizabeth. She married Charles Dimsdale whose father, the late John Dimsdale, an amateur rider, killed at Huntingdon, was owner of Parasol, a top class hunter chaser.

Bruce began the 1967 season with sixty horses in two yards. He had come a long way and achieved much since riding into the limelight on Battleship at Aintree in 1938.

We sat together one evening before dinner after a successful day at Yarmouth and discussed this fine trainer's career. He told me, 'I have no regrets about any job I have done. One cannot learn too much. When I hear young trainers after eighteen months' or two years' experience saying that they know how to train horses I am really amazed.'

Bruce is fortunate in having a steady supply of potentially high class horses, not only from his fellow directors, but from the studs of owner-breeders such as Sir Kenneth and Lady Butt, Mrs de Rothschild, Sir Thomas Pilkington, Lord Fairhaven, Arthur Budgett and several others. He buys fifteen or more horses a year for his patrons. He goes to all the yearling sales in England and sometimes to Ireland. He says, 'People can be critical of the yearlings offered at the Doncaster St Leger sales. I like to go there because one gets one's eye in and there are nice horses to be bought if you take your time. This has been proved.'

I asked Bruce if he bought yearlings by appearance or pedigree. He replied, 'In my opinion conformation is ninety-nine per cent of the business. No! The stud book doesn't matter as much as people think. If the yearling looks right to my eye, then if the pedigree fits, I'll bid for that one. In fact I take a chance with a horse with a moderate pedigree if I like his looks.'

'Do you believe in getting a move on with your two-year-olds?' I asked Bruce.

'No, I don't. I cannot force horses. In fact I don't usually have a two year-old winner till the second Newmarket meeting—the Guineas meeting.'

'Do you like any particular type of horse? A potential sprinter or a likely stayer?'

Back came his reply. 'I am not fussy what distance really.

When buying horses, once I've found the individual and the pedigree fits, I don't mind whether it's a sprinter or a stayer so long as I've got the right sort of customer for that animal. Very often I buy horses on my own, but if I have a specific order to fill, well then it may not be quite so easy. I may have found something else which I like, then I ring up the commissioner and say, "I am sorry I haven't got quite what you wanted but in my opinion this is a particularly nice horse and I should think he will be a winner." Well, nine times out of ten they say, "All right, have a go".'

When I asked Bruce to name some of the horses which have given him the most pleasure to train he was at first cautious. 'A lot of horses have given me a lot of pleasure,' he said. 'I'm told I have got a name for being a good judge of a yearling. I hate spending big money on them. I've only done that once, and I don't regret it. The horse was Eve Lady Rosebery's Crested Grebe, by Blakeney, which won as a two-year-old beating twenty-three rivals over a mile at Sandown. He cost 40,000 guineas.

'I suppose Hot Foot is a horse which has given me particular pleasure. He was the first horse I bought for Tony Villar and his mother, Betty Fyfe-Jameson. I paid three thousand five hundred quid for him. He won a lot of good races for us. He also sired Hot Grove, second in the Derby, and Tachypous, second in the Two Thousand Guineas.' (Hot Foot was syndicated after his racing career for £120,000—not bad for a 3,500 guineas yearling.)

'Hot Foot was not easy to train. He was a Firestreak,' said Bruce. 'I am a great believer in knowing the characteristics of sire and dam. I look for them the whole time coming out in their offspring's conformation and behaviour.

'The Firestreaks and Pardals for instance. Some of them are inclined to be back at the knee. Some also are a tiny bit highly strung. As long as the mares down the female tail line of a pedigree are not too hot, then one has got a very good chance of training the offspring.' (It is only fair to mention that Firestreak has sired many winners including Snow Knight, hero of the 1974 Derby. Pardal, a stallion of world repute, sired Firestreak.)

'Another one which gave me great pleasure to train was a little filly for which I paid 1,250 guineas. She was Catherine Wheel,

South African jockey John Gorton wins the P.T.S. Laurels Stakes on Mr Tony Villar's Hotfoot, Goodwood 1970. (Sport & General)

the first horse I bought for Tom Blackwell. She was third in the One Thousand Guineas, won the Musidora Stakes at York, the New Ham Stakes and Nassau Stakes at Goodwood, and other races. Touch Paper won a Goodwood Stewards' Cup for us. I bought him at Doncaster for very little money. In my view it is unnecessary to spend millions to be successful. Most people expect to get their money back if they spend scores of thousands of pounds on a yearling. Well, it just doesn't happen that way as a rule, in this business.

175

'Take a Reef was another very good horse we bought cheaply. I don't take the credit for buying him on my own. I was helped there. He was top of the three-year-old Free Handicap.'

When Jack Jarvis died Doug Smith took over the Rosebery horses. Doug won the Oaks with sleeping Partner for Lord Rosebery and it was some two years later that Bruce got a call. Would he take over Lord Rosebery's horses? In many ways Bruce was glad to have them but it meant that he had about a hundred horses to train and three yards to supervise—Park Lodge, Palace House and Albert House.

'I like to get round all my horses at least once a day, I do still.' So it meant that with the Rosebery horses Bruce had really got more than enough on his plate.

Chil the Kite was the outstanding horse which he bought for Lady Rosebery at the dispersal sale. Bruce did well with him before the horse was shipped to America. 'I suppose Jolly Good was one of the best horses I've trained. He won the Magnet Cup, the White Rose Stakes and the Peter Hastings Stakes. But it's hard to say which is the best horse I have trained. I've been very fortunate. I could bracket six or seven together I suppose. Yes, I've had some very good horses since I have been here at Palace House. Stilvi, for instance, a very fast filly and dam of Tachypous. She cost 6,200 guineas and was the second horse I bought for George Cambanis. As a three-year-old, ridden by John Gorton, she won the Duke of York Stakes at Sandown, and the King George Stakes at Goodwood.

'Tom Cribb, one of the Rosebery horses, was a great challenge because he was savage but he was a blooming good horse. And don't forget Grey Baron, winner of the Goodwood Cup. Everything was right for him that day. He was fit and well and the ground was just right. Now there's a horse I bought for 2,800 guineas. A very cheap horse. A bit of luck. But there you are . . .

'The only classic I've won is the Swedish St Leger with Royal Park. We were second in the Two Thousand Guineas with Tachypous. We have also had horses placed in the St Leger and in the Guineas here and in Ireland several times.'

*   *   *

I asked Bruce if he could remember any dramas during his career. To give me an example he went back to his days at Freemason Lodge with Sir Cecil Boyd-Rochfort.

Let him introduce the story in his own words: 'Always before a classic we had a night watchman or two to keep an eye on the place. You know, an ante-nobbling watch. Old Jack Dawes who I now meet on the weighing-room door at Yarmouth had the job. The sitting-up room for him was the best tack room which was right next door to the cottage which Betty and I had.'

On that morning Bruce heard a knock on the wall. He got up.

'Yes, Jack?' Bruce enquired. 'What's the matter?'

'Alcide's gone,' Jack replied.

'What?!!!!!'

'Alcide's gone,' Jack said again. Alcide was the St Leger favourite.

So Bruce turned out quickly. On the landing was a window from which he could look down the bottom yard at Freemason Lodge.

'I took a quick shufti through it and there to my astonishment and delight was Alcide hobnobbing with the fillies over the box doors,' Bruce related. 'We caught him and put him in his box. He was none the worse.'

It was six o'clock on a Sunday morning. Bruce rang Fred Day, the vet, straight away. He told him that Alcide had been loose and that The Captain had not been informed as it was so early. He asked Fred if he would be good enough to come up as soon as possible and 'run his rule over' the colt.

Bruce went on: 'I did not think there was anything wrong with Alcide but I naturally wanted Fred's confirmation of this so that when The Captain got up I could tell him what had happened and what action I had taken. I explained this to Fred. Up he came and confirmed that the colt was one hundred per cent all right.'

Bruce went over to the house at seven o'clock to see The Captain. The first person he saw was old Tom Woollard, the gardener. A great character. He was getting the coal in. Said Tom, 'You won't get HIM up yet.'

'Won't I? You'll soon see. Where's the bloody bell? I'll get him out,' Bruce replied with quiet fervour.

Down came The Captain. 'What's the matter, Hobbs? What's the matter?'

'Nothing to alarm you Sir, but I must tell you that your phone is going to ring shortly and you ought to know why.' So Bruce put him in the picture and wound up with 'the horse is perfectly all right'.

'Oh! Thank God! Thank God!' said the trainer. And off he went. Not long after that his phone began to ring. As Bruce commented, it is impossible to keep things quiet for long in Newmarket.

How did it happen? All Bruce would say was, 'There were one or two real villains about in those days.'

Bruce then turned to the subject of 'staff'. 'I have got, without fear of contradiction, one of the best head men in the country. I think he is the best. His name is Ted Molyneux and he has been with me for twelve years. He was with me one year at Robinson's and came here with me. He is a brilliant feeder, a very good organiser and we refer to him affectionately as "Nanny" because he is so good at nursing—horses, of course. He is completely and utterly reliable. He is back at work with me after a serious heart attack. As a result of this I have taken on an assistant. Normally I don't like this because they will not always work as I had to do. But I was lucky in finding a very good chap, Bill Mather, who gets on with Molyneux. That's important because anyone I have as an assistant must get on with Molyneux. An assistant must not come between us. Anyway Bill does not and that's super.

'When Brian Lunness left me he said, "Guv'nor, I'll find you a replacement as travelling head lad." He has got to be as good as you,' I told him. Lunness was as good as his word. He found me the right chap. He is still with me. Frank Crozier is his name and he is first rate. He was also with Mr Robinson.'

The brilliant Cry of Truth trained by Bruce Hobbs, ridden by John Gorton, wins the William Hill Cheveley Park Stakes, Newmarket 1974. (Sport & General)

I commented to Bruce that he had a very effective and experienced stable jockey in Geoff Lewis. 'Yes, I think he is a very good rider and a great character,' agreed Bruce, adding 'He is a great man for the big occasion.' Bruce also uses Geoff Baxter who he thinks is a very under-rated pilot. Baxter has ridden some outstandingly good races for the stable.

'I have also got a top class apprentice—Compton Rodrigues,' Bruce reminded me. 'This lad is named after the famous cricketer Denis Compton. In 1977 Rodrigues was out of the limelight because he broke a leg in the summer when he was leading apprentice. He is an excellent boy, light and talented. If all goes well with him he will be in the top ten jockeys one day.'

Not surprisingly Rodrigues was back in the winner's enclosure early in the 1978 season.

Another jockey, also a great help to Bruce Hobbs, was the South African John Gorton, brought to England by Lord Rosebery and who rode Sleeping Partner in the Oaks. I shall never forget the look on this young man's face on that occasion as he paused for a few seconds, his feet out of the stirrups, before dismounting in Epsom's winner's circle. His expression was one of quiet and controlled pleasure. For a moment I thought that in his great joy he had forgotten what to do next! In fact he was savouring one of the historic moments in his life and giving the photographers every chance!

John rode 155 winners for Bruce. Among them were Hotfoot in his very successful four-year-old-career and the two brilliant fillies: Lady Butt's Jacinth, bred by the William Hill Studs, and Cry of Truth, bred by her owner Miss Pearl Lawson-Johnston. Both fillies won the Cheveley Park Stakes decisively. Jacinth made an absolutely top class three-year-old over a mile. She started at odds on for the One Thousand Guineas but had the misfortune to find one too good for her in the Noel Murless-trained Mysterious. This classic was Jacinth's first race of the season and it is quite probable that it came slightly too soon for her. At all events Bruce showed his skill as a trainer by carrying off the Coronation Stakes, the Falmouth Stakes and the Goodwood Mile with Jacinth. She was runner-up to the hot favourite Thatch in her only other race of 1973, the Sussex Stakes. She was by Red God, out

180

A runaway victory for Jacinth and another Cheveley Park triumph for Bruce Hobbs and John Gorton. (Sport & General)

of Jaffa, who although not owned by the Butts' Brook Stud of which my father Eric was a director for many years, was bred there and sold as a yearling to the late William Hill for 3,000 guineas. Sir Kenneth Butt paid 16,500 guineas on behalf of the Brook Stud for Jacinth as a yearling from the William Hill Stud's draft at the Houghton Sales, thus returning the blood to the stud.

Now, just one little story which shows how a trainer's wife can help to promote the well-being and success of her husband's stable. Betty Hobbs told me, 'I became very fond of Stilvi, winner of three good two-year-old races including the National Stakes in 1971. We had the most wonderful affinity which started in a very simple way. I often go round the yard after lunch—before the nags have their kip—just talking to them through the bars. After a time Stilvi would always neigh when she heard me coming. She used to love to see me. As she was going to live at Pat McCalmont's stud where Hotfoot lives—he was another of my favourites—I mentioned to Bruce that if Stilvi's owner, Mr Cambanis, agreed, then what a great opportunity for a "marriage of convenience", if the blood lines were right. They were. The result was Tachypous, winner of the Middle Park Stakes.'

Stilvi carries the Hobbs story into 1978. She is the dam of Tromos, by Busted. Speaking of this impressive colt at the time of the Dewhurst Stakes in October, Bruce made no secret of his hopes for this half-brother to Tachypous (by Hotfoot) and Taxiarchos (by Brigadier Gerard) : 'He has always looked to me as if he would be a decent horse. In fact he is potentially a very high class horse and likely to be a real Two Thousand Guineas prospect. He is bigger than his half-brothers and is a very kind horse so long as you treat him kindly—just like his dam. Upset them and they get into a right old panic. No, there's nothing wrong with him.'

Tromos, ridden by Kipper Lynch, won the Clarence House Stakes at Ascot on 23rd September by ten lengths from Milford. His next appearance was in the Dewhurst Stakes (7 f) in which he made all the running easily to beat More Light and Warmington.

Apart from a few outstanding successes 1978 was a most frustrating season for Bruce. 'My horses went wrong in March with virus trouble and it was not until August that I was able to get the two-year-olds right.'

Tumbledownwind went wrong before the Guineas in which he ran the race of his life and then went to pieces. Another casualty was Grey Baron who would have run well in the Ascot Gold Cup. Bruce claims that he was a better horse on the form book than Shangamuzo, winner of the Ascot race. Taxiarchos and Royal Harmony also went wrong. 'Those are the good horses, not to mention the lesser lights,' went on Bruce. 'At the same time we had our successes. Princess Eboli kept her form all through the season and ran well in most of the top staying fillies' races. She won the Cheshire Oaks and the Lancashire Oaks and don't forget that before Taxiarchos went wrong he won three times including a defeat of Homing (received 8 lb) at Sandown. We also won a £15,000 race at Hamburg with Roscoe Blake and he was only three lengths behind Trillion, the Arc de Triomphe second, at Cologne. Roscoe Blake must have give in the ground.'

This colt stays in training in 1979. According to his trainer he has a wonderful temperament. It is as well to remember that his dam is Rhodie, who foaled Jolly Good, sent out to win top races by Bruce.

With the departure of Geoff Lewis who rode so successfully for several years for the stable, Bruce engaged John ('Kipper') Lynch as the stable jockey. Bruce's comment on this was, 'If my owners want to pick and choose who rides then they will do so. Kipper understands that, but he'll get a lot of riding for me and if he gets on well with a horse then I shall do my best to see that he is not taken off him. He has ridden winners in nine different countries. I think he will suit me,' he concluded. 'I admire him for the way he has pulled himself up from the floor.'

STATISTICAL RECORDS

Bruce Hobbs has had 15 seasons as a flat race trainer, and 6 seasons training under N.H. Rules. He trained winners of 35 jump races between 1945 and 1951, and 617 winners of £907,449 under Jockey Club Rules (1964–1978).

TRAINERS' TABLE

1970	11th	33 winners of	£39,354
1972	6th	55 winners of	£72,938
1973	9th	53 winners of	£80,155
1974	8th	45 winners of	£86,721
1975	7th	57 winners of	£78,446
1976	6th	55 winners of	£144,080
1977	6th	65 winners of	£157,438
1978	12th	43 winners of	£131,136

BIG RACES

He has trained the winners of approximately 220 races worth more than £1,000 to the winner.

The races worth £4,000 or more to the winner were:

1965

BLUE RIBAND	Epsom	Cambridge	£4,556

1970

| PTS LAURELS | Goodwood | Hotfoot | 4,703 |

1971

| NASSAU | Goodwood | Catherine Wheel | 4,231 |

1972

| CHEVELEY PARK | Newmarket | Jacinth | 13,711 |

1973

PRINCESS ELIZABETH	Epsom	Mystic Circle	4,167
CORONATION STAKES	Royal Ascot	Jacinth	9,534
JOE CORAL NORTHUMBERLAND	Newcastle	Tom Cribb	8,502
FALMOUTH	Newmarket	Jacinth	4,258
GOODWOOD MILE	Goodwood	Jacinth	4,191
GORDON	Goodwood	Duke of Ragusa	4,345

1974

CHESTER VASE	Chester	Jupiter Pluvius	5,132
JOHN SMITH'S MAGNET CUP	York	Take a Reef	4,358
CHEVELEY PARK	Newmarket	Cry of Truth	26,083

1975

| JOCKEY CLUB STAKES | Newmarket | Shebeen | 4,117 |

184

CHERRY HINTON	Newmarket	Everything Nice	£5,219
JOHN SMITH'S MAGNET BOWL	York	Jolly Good	5,042
PETER HASTINGS	Newbury	Jolly Good	4,740

1976

EARL OF SEFTON	Newmarket	Chil the Kite	4,830
WESTBURY	Sandown	Jolly Good	4,552
MUSIDORA	York	Everything Nice	6,107
JERSEY	Royal Ascot	Gwent	6,650
TENNENT TROPHY	Ayr	Grey Baron	8,103
WM HILL MIDDLE PARK	Newmarket	Tachypous	33,383

1977

CHESHIRE OAKS	Chester	Brightly	7,479
JOHN OF GAUNT	Haydock	Gwent	7,694
HENRY II	Sandown	Grey Baron	6,840
JULY STAKES	Newmarket	Royal Harmony	16,153
GOODWOOD CUP	Goodwood	Grey Baron	10,111
GIMCRACK	York	Tumbledownwind	26,178
JOCKEY CLUB CUP	Newmarket	Grey Baron	8,880

1978

CHESHIRE OAKS	Chester	Princess Eboli	8,260
LANCASHIRE OAKS	Haydock	Princess Eboli	12,665
LAND OF BURNS	Ayr	Taxiarchos	5,676
EGLINTON AND WINTON	Ayr	Epilogue	4,253
WM HILL DEWHURST	Newmarket	Tromos	33,950

Valuable place money in big races in 1978:

4th	Two Thousand Guineas	Newmarket	Tumbledownwind	£4,431
2nd	Gus Demmy	Haydock	Tumbledownwind	2,056
2nd	Diomed	Epsom	Gwent	4,177
2nd	Gordon Stakes	Goodwood	Roscoe Blake	4,219
3rd	Parkhill	Doncaster	Princess Eboli	2,518

BEST RACECOURSES

Newmarket	93	wins
Yarmouth	46	,,
Goodwood	30	,,
Lingfield	29	,,
Ascot	27	,,
York	27	,,
Leicester	27	,,
Nottingham	25	,,
Wolverhampton	25	,,
Kempton	24	,,

Eight Flat-Racing Stables

JOCKEYS

John Gorton	155 wins
Geoff Lewis	150 ,,
Stan Clayton	51 ,,
Geoff Baxter	45 ,,
Paul Cook	24 ,,
Willie Snaith	16 ,,
Joe Mercer	14 ,,
Compton Rodrigues	14 ,,
David East	10 ,,
Edward Hide	9 ,,

BEST MONTHS

August	111 wins
July	108 ,,
September	103 ,,
June	97 ,,

A plateau more than a peak. He has averaged approximately 45 winners a season. Best season for winners and stakes: 1977: 65 wins £157,438.

MULTIPLE WINS

He has had one four-timer on 30th July 1977 (Goodwood and treble at Newmarket) and 64 doubles, of which six straight doubles at Newmarket and Yarmouth, plus five multiple wins and four mixed doubles involving Newmarket, and one multiple win and six mixed doubles involving Yarmouth.

FIRST WINNERS TRAINED

Jumping: Devon Glory, Cheltenham, Division I of Shurdington November Handicap (£136) 2 m. Owned Mrs J. Rogerson, ridden G. Archibald. Friday, 21st December 1945.

Flat: Ward Drill, Newmarket, Blue Peter Stakes. 5 f—two-year-old maidens at starting. Owned David Robinson, ridden Harry Carr. Saturday, 16th May 1964.

HORSES

Wandering Eyes which he trained for Mr David Robinson and took with him when he trained on his own account, won eight races between 1964–9. Absolved won eight races between 1969–72. Royal Park won in '71, '72, '73. Shebeen won in '73, '74, '75. Chil the Kite won in '74, '75, '76.

186

OWNERS

Mr and Mrs John Rogerson who gave Bruce his start as a trainer under
N.H. Rules also supported him when he turned to the Flat. He trained
19 Flat winners for the late Mrs Rogerson and has trained several for
Mr Rogerson.

He trained 33 winners for Mrs J. Bricken from 1966 to 1974. Other
consistent winning owners, the majority of which figure currently:
H. D. H. Wills, J. P. Philipps, A. Villar, T. F. Blackwell, Lord Fairhaven, J. Hambro, George Cambanis, Sir Kenneth Butt, Lord Rosebery
and Eve Lady Rosebery.

RACES FARMED

ROUS MEMORIAL, Goodwood	1973, 1975, 1977
GOODWOOD CUP, Goodwood	1969, 1977
CHAMPION TWO-YEAR-OLD, Ripon	1974, 1976
MUSIDORA, York	1971, 1976
PRINCESS ROYAL, Ascot	1974, 1975
JOHN SMITH'S MAGNET CUP, York	1974, 1975
CHERRY HINTON, Newmarket	1970, 1975
ESHER CUP, Epsom	1973, 1975
YELLOW PAGES, Thirsk	1972, 1973
CHESHIRE OAKS, Chester	1977, 1978

Since the Palace House racing company was formed in the autumn of
1965 (see text), Bruce Hobbs has turned out 579 winners of £898,830.
This sum plus place stakes takes this trainer's total to approximately
£1,200,000.

Peter Walwyn

of Seven Barrows, Lambourn

Peter Walwyn was born on 1st July 1933, son of Colonel Taffy Walwyn, a regular soldier in the Royal Horse Artillery who was awarded a D.S.O. and M.C. in World War I.

In his comfortable, friendly home, Seven Barrows, a mile or two outside Lambourn, Peter told me about this exceptional man and the influence he had on his life. He said of his father: 'He was asked, after he had retired, why he had not become a general? He replied that when he went to his Staff College interview, he told them what he thought they ought to know and not what they wanted to know!

'He was a very, very, good horseman. He rode winners in America and Germany. He also rode a lot of winners in England as an amateur including the 1920 Grand Military Gold Cup on Admiral of the Fleet Sir Hedworth Meux's White Surrey. He was a great show-jumping rider as well and started the British Show Jumping Association. At the end of the war he was largely instrumental in bringing about the foundation of the School of Equitation at Weeden.'

Colonel Walwyn's view was that there ought to be a combined Army Training School for horsemen instead of, at that time, a School for the Cavalry at Netheravon and a Royal Artillery Riding Establishment at Woolwich. Having put up this idea—it was approved—he followed it quickly with another. He requested to be made the first chief instructor at Weeden. That was also agreed!

'When he retired he went racing quite a bit,' Peter told me.

'As a schoolboy I used to go with him to Cheltenham. I became mad about racing. Fulke Walwyn, my first cousin—our fathers were brothers—was my idol, and still is. He is twenty-three years older than I am and there is no doubt that he is a very great trainer. I used to take *Raceform* when I was at school at Charterhouse and of course I set my heart on going into racing one day.'

Colonel Walwyn knew one of racing's great men of the Forties and Fifties, Mr Geoffrey Freer, the senior handicapper. He promised to do what he could to help Peter, and got in touch with the Newmarket trainer Geoffrey Brooke to see if he would take the young man as an assistant.

'So that's where I went. I was at Clarehaven for three years,' Peter said. 'I did everything from travelling the horses to being head lad in charge of what was called "the bottom yard". I learned a great deal. It was fascinating being at Newmarket. Having been trained there one realises what a lot of advantages the place has. The gallops are looked after, and you just have to read on the notice board which gallops are open and which are shut. And there you are. As a downland trainer with my own ground I have to say, I'll use this bit today and shut it up tomorrow! It's one more responsibility.'

Having been at Newmarket for three years Peter wanted to broaden his experience. He was in luck in this respect. Mrs Helen Johnson Houghton, sister of Fulke Walwyn, and therefore another first cousin, wrote to Peter and said that Charles Jerdein who held the licence for her was giving up and would he—Peter—go and help her at Blewbury? ' "Marvellous", I said, and joined Helen. I held the licence for four years in the later 1950s and early 1960s.' During that short time Helen trained more than a hundred winners.

It was in the mid-1950s that the Jockey Club first permitted women to hold a trainer's licence. Before that there were of course several women trainers, but they had to get a man to hold the licence. Sometimes the man was only the figurehead. In other instances he was a genuine hard working partner in the enterprise, as was Peter. Helen, one of the first women to be a member of the Jockey Club, was exceptional in that she did not apply for a licence although she could have done so.

'When I went to Helen's stable there were about twenty

horses, not particularly good ones at that. Poor woman, she was at a low ebb having lost her husband, Gordon, in a hunting accident and having in the past had such good horses as Gilles de Retz, the Guineas winner and also Nucleus. That was the horse, ridden by Lester Piggott, which very nearly beat Meld, who was suffering from a temperature, in the 1955 St Leger.

As might be expected, Helen Johnson Houghton and Geoffrey Brooke were Peter's chief mentors. 'I learned a tremendous amount from them,' Peter told me. 'But training at Newmarket and being head lad in the "bottom yard" at Clarehaven for a year differed greatly from my work at Blewbury. I'll try to tell you why.

'Mr Brooke was a most marvellous man. He and his wife Betty were wonderful people to work for. And *work* was the operative word. Quite rightly I worked very hard. We tidied up the bottom yard. When I went there first it was a sea of mud. We put gravel down and made lawns which I used to mow in the afternoons.

' "The Guvnor" had little fillies there. His policy was to get them really fit, win races with them as two-year-olds and then sell them. There was no question of allowing them lots of time to develop although of course he was patient with some. Most of them were little rats of things bought at the sales for little money and then—zip!

Peter Walwyn, whose great success as a trainer in the Sixties and Seventies has been one of the outstanding features of the British Turf.

'As I have said, there was not much of these fillies. We used to go round feeding them at mid-day in an attempt to build them up a bit. Some of them would eat only a mere handful of oats, mixed with some carrots and grass in the daytime. The better ones would win a couple of races in the spring. Doug Smith rode them. He was a superb jockey, particularly on two-year-olds. I don't mean to say that "The Guvnor" had only sharp little fillies in his yard. He always had some very nice youngsters, but as you will understand these were not handled in quite the same way.

'All this was a great education. It was a humming place. Geoffrey had a marvellous head lad called Bob Ruttle, who is still a great friend of mine. I see him when I go to Newmarket. He would agree with me that Mr Brooke was a perfectionist. Just to show you what I thought of him I can say now that I would love to go back to him for a refresher course and be sharpened up—to re-learn what I have forgotten about stable management. It was a very, very well run place.'

Peter learned from Geoffrey but Helen taught him a tremendous amount as well. She has always been a superb judge of a yearling and a marvellous placer of horses. They got on extremely well and were acknowledged to be a great partnership. 'She is a splendid person,' said Peter. 'She has had a lot of bad luck, but she has battled on marvellously. Her husband Gordon was only about fifty when he was killed. Sadly I never met him. But he was in the top flight of trainers and one gathers that he was sure to have been leading trainer.'

Not only did Peter learn from Helen about placing horses, but also about bringing them on slowly. It was probably her aim to make horses improve all the time if she could. Undoubtedly she was a fantastic trainer of horses and her knowledge of them is extensive.

As has already been made plain, Geoffrey Brooke's was a very commercial set-up. He did have some owner-breeders, but the majority of his horses were bought to run, win and sell—then re-invest. As an observer of the racing scene I believe that the Brooke policy, seen at first hand by the young Walwyn, has been an important factor in the now mature trainer's successful career. He has good contacts with leading bloodstock agencies and is not

Happy faces encircle Grundy as he is led in by his owner Dr Carlos Vittadini after winning the Derby. Peter Walwyn in black topper looks over jockey Pat Eddery's shoulder.

slow to advise owners to exploit the commercial possibilities of their horses. It would be wrong to say that Peter's policy is one of buying two-year-olds 'to run, win, sell and re-invest', but the fact remains that the successful trainer today is—has to be—an enterprising businessman, which Geoffrey Brooke was. There is not the slightest doubt that Peter has adapted Geoffrey's example to suit his own style and standard of training.

'The fascinating thing was that at Newmarket the horses got a lot more work than those I helped train at Blewbury,' Peter told me. 'The Newmarket horses did more fast work. On the Blewbury hills we did not do much galloping. What is interesting to me is that we do even less fast work here at Lambourn than we did at Blewbury. The whole thing is due to terrain. For instance we have a canter past the house here which is like a precipice—well, it's very steep! The horses go very steady up it. It's good for the wind.

192

'In 1959,' Peter recalls, 'I met Virginia my wife, who is a sister of Nick Gaselee, the trainer. "Bonk", as we call her, came from Kent. We got married. In due course I said to Helen that I didn't think that I could go on in my job with her unless I had a chance of taking over the stable. Well, there was little hope of that because Helen's son Fulke was growing up and was destined to hold the licence. I thought it was time I branched off and started training on my own. I gave Helen a year's notice. During that time Bonk and I lived in a very small cottage. We nosed around a bit and eventually bought Windsor House, Lambourn, in 1960, from Sid Mercer. It had thirty boxes, eleven acres, two cottages, and a very nice house. It cost us £12,000. What it would have cost today I don't know. Fortunately I had a little capital. My mother and father died in the year we got married and one of the reasons why I wanted to set up on my own was that I wanted to use my capital wisely.'

Peter's mother, Alexandra, had bought him his Blewbury cottage. He sold that and also his parents' home at Chastleton, near Moreton-in-the-Marsh, Gloucestershire. So he was lucky to have a bit of money with which to start training. He didn't know quite what his next step should be so he consulted Dick Poole, who was a good friend of the Johnson Houghtons and the Walwyns. He said to Dick, 'I look like starting training. I don't know any owners at all. What do you think I ought to do?' Dick advised Peter to find a place and start. 'Fine,' said Peter, sticking to his point, 'but who will send me any horses?' Dick was most encouraging and told him that owners and horses would appear all right.

'To give meaning to his words he was the first man to send me a horse,' Peter said. 'He has still got horses with me. Evelyn de Rothschild was another of my original owners and so was Charles Smith-Bingham. They are still with me.

'Dick Poole's chief advice, which I don't know that I have carried out completely, was: "If possible you should choose owners who wear a hat and a tie". Most of mine actually do wear hats and ties! We can laugh at that now but that advice was given to me in 1961, and things have changed a bit since then.'

*   *   *

The staff at Seven Barrows lined up behind Peter and his wife Virginia. (Daily Mirror/Syndication International)

Peter's first winner was a horse called Don Verde, over hurdles at Worcester in the autumn of 1960. The horse was owned by Martin Dunne, son of Captain Philip Dunne, who had some very good horses including Bellacose, a sprinter. Martin Dunne is still very interested in racing but he has given up owning and is Master of the Warwickshire Hounds. Don Verde won three times over hurdles and was ridden for Peter by John Oaksey.

'The poor horse broke his neck at Cheltenham,' Peter related sadly. 'We were able to get him into a horsebox and hoped we would get him home, but he died during the journey. It was a shattering thing to happen. We felt it particularly keenly as he was our first winner.'

The following year, 1961, saw Peter launched as a trainer on the Flat, and his first winner also came at Worcester. It was in May that he saddled Brigadier Wyndham Torr's filly Snaefell (100 to 7) to win the Bedwardine Handicap (1 m). She was ridden by Greville Starkey.

Then Peter made a revealing remark and one which somehow struck a chord in my own mind: 'Every winner is a miracle really. Even now when we have a lot more winners I always think it is a great excitement. The thrill never wears off.'

About 1964 Peter was riding down the road on an old horse called Flambeau, when he met Derek Candy's string at exercise. Mrs Candy was walking beside him and as they passed Seven Barrows, where David Hastings trained, Mrs Candy said to him, 'Would you like to train there?' Peter said he couldn't afford it, but that he would love to. He didn't know at that time that Seven Barrows was owned by the Candys who lived at Kingstone Warren. Mrs Candy told him that it could be on the market quite soon. Then Peter realised the full strength of her remarks and said, 'If it is ever on the market would you please consider giving me first refusal? I don't know what it would cost and I don't know what is involved but I would be interested.'

The following summer Mr and Mrs Candy approached Peter in the paddock at Wolverhampton, and told him that Seven Barrows was coming on the market shortly, and that he had first refusal. He didn't know what to do about it because he didn't know where the money was coming from. He fancied the place very much. What appealed to him was that it was out of the village of Lambourn and that it had got its own gallops. In fact at that time Peter was using them, thanks to the kindness of David Hastings. David leased Seven Barrows from the Candys who had bought the place as part of a package deal from the Craven Estates in 1960.

In the spring of 1965 the Candys' lawyer wrote to Peter and said, 'Seven Barrows is for sale and the price is so and so. We are offering it to you privately because the Candys would like you to have it and we would like to sell it as soon as we conveniently can.'

Peter and Bonk had to make up their minds quickly. They decided to buy. They spent about a year adding to the buildings and altering them. According to Peter they have not stopped doing that ever since. But first of all they had to get the house right and build a hostel and cottages for the lads.

At that time Peter had been worried that at Windsor House, if he wanted to expand, which he did, the place had no scope at all. Friends like David Hastings and Bob Reed let him use their gallops, but it was very much a cap-in-hand business. They were very good to him, but he wanted to have his own place with its own facilities. Now he and Bonk own four hundred acres.

Peter and Bonk moved into Seven Barrows at the end of 1965. Incidentally I don't suppose I am the first man to ask why he called his charming wife by such an unusual and abrupt name. 'She has always been called Bonk,' Peter told me, 'and I don't really know how it all started. But the great thing about having a wife called Bonk is that if anyone says "Where is Bonk?" you know exactly who they mean.'

Peter then went on: 'I have mentioned some of my early owners already, but of course I simply must include Mr Percival Williams, for many years Master of the Four Burrow Foxhounds. He was owner of Be Hopeful and he offered me the horse in the summer of 1960 when I was about to start training. I know Be Hopeful was not our first winner, but he did win twenty-seven races and we were very fond of the horse. I suppose he did as much as any other animal in the yard to get us going. Later on I trained Mabel, a good filly, for him, also Pasty, winner of the Cheveley Park

Stakes (1975). She was named after a good foxhound bitch in the Four Burrow pack and a winner at Peterborough Show. Another of my original owners was Charles Benson, now The Scout of the *Daily Express*. He always wore a collar and tie and sometimes even a hat! He and the Masters, parents of Carol, Charlie's first wife, sent me a horse or two. The kindness of these few friends gave us a footing.'

Peter has a number of owner-breeders among his patrons so he has a steady stream of well bred youngsters coming to his yard. He also buys regularly and does this with the co-operation of agents such as Robin Hastings of the British Bloodstock Agency, or Keith Freeman who 'found' Grundy for Peter's patron, Dr Carlo Vittadini.

Peter observed, 'I think it is a help to have an agent, because they have more time than I have for the finding of horses. Once the season starts life is one mad rush. I dash off racing on a Monday and tell the agent that I'll meet him before the first lot is offered at Newmarket on Tuesday morning. I find I have not got the time to spend two or three days beforehand looking round yearlings, but I do of course study the catalogue and ask the agent to look at the yearlings I have picked out as possibilities.'

When Peter arrives at the sale he meets his agent and probably says, 'Now come on, what have you seen that's nice?' Peter's owners also have lists of the lots he is interested in.

'We compare notes the whole time,' Peter said. 'We go round and see the ones I have got on my list and sort them out. It's continual discussion. There is background work to see if any of the previous foals out of a mare have won, what their Timeform rating was, whether they were nice animals, whether they trained on and made good mature horses—all that sort of thing goes into it.

'I train for the Hue-Williams, Perceval Williams, June McCalmont and Louis Freedman who very seldom buy an animal. One knows quite a lot about the yearlings they send in from their studs because one has not only trained their dams but probably their grand-dams. One knows the background of the family and that can sometimes be more than half the battle when it comes to winning races.'

Peter helps some of his owner-breeders with their plans. One of these, Louis Freedman, is also greatly helped with his breeding by Peter Willett who is not only an expert but has a facility for writing entertainingly on the subject in the *Sporting Chronicle* and *Horse and Hound*.

'All this is fascinating and good fun,' Peter Walwyn told me. 'If requested I give my opinion about stallions, and how I think a particular stallion will suit a certain mare. I think one is always trying to breed a classic winner, because that's where the enormous money lies.

'You have got to make every horse as good as it can be, but so much luck does come into breeding. I'll give you an example: I was visiting Newmarket one day. I saw John Waugh who was training then, sitting on his hack. The animal was by Nimbus, winner of the Two Thousand Guineas and the Derby, and was out of Zabara, winner of the One Thousand Guineas. It didn't look much and John said that on a racecourse it was absolutely useless.'

I next asked Peter one of my stock questions. 'Would you say that appearance—a horse that fills your eye—interests you more than pedigree?'

'It's a lot of both. The thing is you can "get out of" a horse with a good pedigree if he is a reasonable racehorse, better than you can "get out of" a winning racehorse with no pedigree. Obviously the useless horse with no pedigree is hopeless to sell.'

Peter then continued to comment succinctly on make and shape. 'Conformation really means that a horse's action is right. If a horse is straight in front (i.e. has upright pasterns) he is more likely to break down because his shock absorbers are not sufficiently resilient. If he has got bad hocks he may be prone to curbs or thoro' pins. If he has a lengthy, tubular body and runs up light, the odds are he won't stand his work. If he has a ewe neck he is more likely to put his head up when tiring at the end of a race than a horse with a good, forward, well set on neck. If he has little ears it is possible that he will be more ungenuine than a horse with lop ears. I like having one of those because they are usually game.'

Having bought his yearlings and taken in those from his owners' studs, a trainer is then busy breaking them in. When this

199

job is nearing completion Peter begins to divide them into three groups. He explained, 'I say to myself well, those are the early ones. They may not be worth much money or they look small, so I slip them along, trying to win with them and sell them.' This is the method he learned with Geoffrey Brooke. 'Next comes the middle bracket which could include good horses, the possible Ascot two-year-olds and others which we race in July and August. Then you get the backward ones, most of which we bring out in September and October.

'The middle ones probably flow into the backward ones. By that time the early ones, I hope, have won, and are ready to sell. They are the type that will not improve. Once a two-year-old has won three or four races he goes high in the handicap, and it is hard to win more races with him. So I have to develop the sales side. I cannot really afford not to do so. I have so many horses coming in, I've got to say to the owner, "You can sell your horse reasonably well now, and you will have money to buy another yearling, or you can buy a house or make up your drive— just whatever you want to do.

'I have got to keep turning the whole thing over. I don't hang about if a horse is good. For example, I sold a horse the other day that had been placed twice. Pat Eddery, our jockey, said the horse did not always exert himself. We sent him to the sales and he made 5,000 guineas. Not a bad price for a failure. On the other hand he was a two-year-old and he may win a race or two as an older horse, but I think it best to cash in on a horse like that.'

'Let's start at the top,' I suggested to Peter, when asking him to talk about his team of workers. 'There's your wife, Bonk, I know she helps.'

'She is marvellous. Yes, she is a very great help to me,' said Peter. 'She rides extremely well. She is not competitive from the race-riding point of view, but she rides fillies in beautiful work at home. She loves it. (Incidentally, I think it is wrong for the colts to be ridden or looked after by girls.) She is also a very good driver, which takes a lot of pressure off me. She likes being involved in the running of a stable. In fact she is a fellow director of my company. She doesn't actually place the horses—you know,

Humble Duty, a very high class filly, with her trainer Peter and Virginia (Bonk) Walwyn. (Fiona Vigors)

find the right races for them—but she looks after the owners and is concerned with the welfare of all of us here. She adores the life.

'I had a very good head lad called Ray Laing who had several jobs before he came to me seventeen years ago. We started off together and he was excellent at his job. He felt the pressure was getting too much for him and he decided to leave in the spring of 1978, which was a great shock to me because we had worked together so happily for so long. Ray now trains for Tony Stratton Smith who bought Bill Payne's yard in Eastbury, and put him in as trainer. Yes, Ray rose up with me, scratching away, getting to the top. It was sad to lose him.'

Peter promoted Mat McCormack to succeed Ray Laing. He is the man who used to ride Grundy at exercise. Not only is he a top-class rider, but he is an excellent feeder of horses, in which job he is helped by Red Groves and Ron Thomas. Tony Driscoll and Eddie Towell are Peter's travelling head men. He has other men including Barry Payne whom he has no hesitation in sending anywhere with horses. Barry rode a winner or two. His mother runs a riding school and his father rode winners under P.T.C. rules. Peter sums up: 'Not only do we have these key men but we have our own gallop men and secretaries. They all pull together. We have a super team. In my office I have got two marvellous girls,' he enthused. 'They are Christine Stephenson and Sandra Bentinck. Christine is daughter of Willie Stephenson, the Royston trainer, one of the very few men to saddle a Derby and a Grand National winner. She is a damn good secretary and a smashing girl who has been with us for about four years. Sandra is daughter of our local saddler. She does the wages and PAYE and that sort of thing. She works for her father when she is not working here.

'I do the entries every day, in fact I concentrate on them and go through them two or three times. I spend a lot of time thinking about them, and, having done so, I say to one of my office staff "no change with this" or "change that and change this". We are always sifting through our entries. I've got a Telex. That means that you can type something out on it, and push it through to Weatherbys, and therefore have a record of it. There can be no argument. They cannot say, "We did not receive that entry".'

Peter says that he has no bees in his bonnet about feeding. He is a great believer in as much natural food for his horses as possible. That means the best hay and the best Australian oats. They get lucerne cut for them in the summer and clover is cut every day for them. Other items on the menu are honey, linseed, and barley. They are also given certain iron tonics which they need when under pressure.

Among Peter's favourite courses is Salisbury. 'I know it is not a Group 1 course, but I like running my horses there,' he told me. 'It's partly an uphill course. It's what is known as a galloping track and it is of course close to home. Furthermore the going there, in my opinion, is usually pretty good.

'Of course I love Ascot. We are leading stable there by quite

*It looks easy but this Grundy win in the King George VI and Queen
Elizabeth Diamond Stakes from Bustino was the hardest-fought
finish of his career.* (Keystone)

a long way. Again it is close to home. It's a sharpish track in lots of ways but it is a very good one. I think Doncaster is a superb track. It is a wonderful galloping track and the ground there is usually very good. We have been lucky there.'

I drew Peter's attention to the fact that Wolverhampton is one of his most successful courses—fourth in his list and only eight behind Ascot. His comment was, 'It's not a bad track, Wolverhampton. If you run your less good horses there you have a chance of picking up some races. I ran that good filly Pasty there and she won first time out. She won the Cheveley Park Stakes the same year (1975). That was a lucky one. The great thing is if you can win a race with an animal first time out you can always make them improve a bit, and perhaps get to the top. Wolverhampton is the sort of course where one can produce a potentially useful animal to win first time, and don't forget, that once they have won they are worth a bit of money'.

'I suppose the best horse I have trained is Grundy, my 1975 Derby winner. He was a very relaxed horse. A very good horse with plenty of fire and spirit. Whether he was quite a Mill Reef, a Nijinsky or a Sea Bird I don't know, but he was a bloody good horse.'

Peter, who did so wonderfully well with this colt, came quickly to the one comparatively unhappy feature in Grundy's career, his defeat in the Benson and Hedges Gold Cup by Dahlia, the very high class French-trained mare, at York. Peter said, 'I was probably wrong to run him at York after the King George VI and Queen Elizabeth Diamond Stakes in which he ran a super race to beat Bustino. I was tied down. As you know the Levy Board had bought him for the National Stud. I was allowed four more races after the Derby. I was not allowed to run him in the Arc de Triomphe so I said to myself, "Well, what do I do with the horse?" I could have put him in the Champion Stakes of a mile and a quarter in the autumn, but I think by that time the horse would have needed a mile and a half. I thought that I had better keep going with him while he was well. He won the Irish Sweeps Derby, and then he had that very hard race at Ascot with Bustino. There were no other races over one and a half miles at all. He seemed very well after his Ascot race. He had eaten up everything and was jumping and kicking, but you can't tell with these horses.

'It is interesting to recall that I trained him for the Two Thousand Guineas because originally I rated him purely as a Guineas horse. He was beaten, unluckily I think, by Bolkonski, but of course everything from then on was a bonus. He did very well.

'I was hopeful that he would win the Benson and Hedges for although it is less than a mile and a half (the actual distance is one mile two and a half furlongs), it is on a truly galloping and testing course with a long run in.

'Grundy was full of character and a fiery colt, but with no harm in him at all. We never worked him much at home. I did however work him on Henry Candy's gallops. Henry, who as you know, has taken over from his father, has been very good to me with his gallops. It makes a nice change to do a bit of work there. I took Grundy up there before the Irish Sweeps Derby and the

A comfortable Derby win for Grundy from the French-trained Nobiliary, with Hunza Dancer third. (Sport & General)

King George. He didn't impress me at all, and I was rather gloomy. I didn't think he would win either race on those showings. On our own ground Grundy used to lob along behind the others. He was fit, and as he didn't need a lot of work, well, that was just fine.'

Peter then turned to his fillies. His thoughts were at once on Louis Freedman's Lucyrowe who won the Coronation Stakes at Ascot, the Sun Chariot Stakes at Newmarket and two other high class races. 'She was a smashing filly on the racecourse, but she has been a bit disappointing at stud so far, but she has bred a very nice two-year-old filly, Edwinarowe, by Blakeney, still to run. Humble Duty, who won the Cheveley Park Stakes as a two-year-old, and as a three-year-old took the One Thousand Guineas, the Coronation Stakes, the Sussex Stakes and the Wills Mile, was obviously a super filly too. Both were very masculine fillies. While they were trained neither ever came in season. Probably they were all the better for that. As a matter of fact, of the good fillies I have trained, very few have come in season, or been much worry.

'These fillies were not difficult to train. They were just normal fillies in most respects. Basically, you know, you don't want to overtrain fillies. They don't need as much work as colts. They just want keeping happy. They train themselves. When you know they can go, then you give them what training they need. This is where the stable jockey comes in very useful.

'I've been very lucky with jockeys really. When I started training I said to Joe Mercer that I'd like him to ride for me as much as possible. He rode a lot of winners for me. I asked him to leave Dick Hern to come to me, but very loyally he did not do that, although Dick at that time had a couple of very bad years due to the virus sweeping through the yard.'

Peter, when he knew he couldn't get Joe, looked around for a good rider, and as Duncan Keith was out of a job Peter engaged him as first stable jockey.

'Duncan did me very well,' said Peter. 'He was second in the Derby on Linden Tree and also second in the Oaks on Frontier Goddess. I think he would have won the One Thousand Guineas on Humble Duty, but he had weight problems at that time, and so the ride went to Lester Piggott. Keith was not only a good jockey, but a very sound judge of a horse too. He would jump off a horse after one of its early races and in answer to the question, "Is it any good?" he might say, "Yes, it'll win a race, but you have got to go as far north as possible".' Coming from a Scotsman that remark has a certain piquancy.

Duncan rode Rock Roi for the stable. He was a good horse but he hated the firm ground. His trainer described him as typical of the Fair Trial breed with shelly feet. The chief races he won were the Gordon Stakes at Goodwood, the Goodwood and Doncaster Cups, the John Porter Stakes, and the Prix du Cadran. He holds the record for Chester's 1 m 5 f. He also won the Ascot Gold Cup twice but was disqualified.

Peter told me, 'At that time phenylbutazone was a drug we used. In fact everybody seemed to be using it. It was given to horses rather like chocolate biscuits to children! We thought it might help Rock Roi because for the first twenty minutes out of his box in the morning he could only hobble. So we gave him a bit of this stuff and it seemed to loosen him up a little bit. We stopped giving it to him five days before the Gold Cup, which he won. Then of course he was tested as a matter of routine, and his urine sample was found to be positive. Naturally we were all upset and there were the most frightful dramas. I believe that because he was a pure stayer his reactions were sluggish. His metabolism was so slow that the "bute" took longer to get through his system than in a sharper horse. At that time the vets were saying we could use the stuff up to seventy-two hours before a race. Now they say use it not less than seven days before a race. So you see veterinary thinking has changed over the past few years.'

Peter had more to say on this subject: 'Obviously a trainer's job is to get his horses as fit as possible within the Rules of Racing so that he can win races for his owners. A trainer does not want to breach the Rules of Racing because that's wrong, but I think it is right that a trainer should do everything that he possibly can to get a horse fit. Whether you just lead a horse out or gallop him every day it doesn't matter. You have to try to get that horse to the peak of its ability.'

Rock Roi, ridden by Duncan Keith, after finishing first in the 1972 Ascot Gold Cup. He was later disqualified following an objection by Pat Eddery, rider of Erimo Hawk. (Sport & General)

I asked Peter if he thought 'bute' was still widely used in the British Isles. 'It's used by some people, but I think everybody is very frightened of it now. It's used a lot in America. There, in most states, its use is permitted, but you have to declare that you are doing so.

' "Bute" does not in any way kill pain. It eases inflammation which causes pain. I know quite a lot about it because I was so involved in the Jockey Club's enquiries into the "bute" business.'

The conversation turned to that sweet filly Polygamy with which Peter won the 1974 Oaks. 'Not only was she an attractive little thing but very tough as well,' Peter told me. 'I thought her best chance of winning a Classic was in the One Thousand Guineas so I trained her for it. She did well in her work and won Ascot's fillies' trial. She then went to Newmarket where she had a bad run in the Guineas, and although she was flying at the finish she was beaten by a short head by the Queen's Highclere. Then I came home thinking, "Oh dear, I think we have missed the boat and we shall not win a Classic with her". By sheer guts and endurance she did win the Oaks. Eddery was at her all the way round. I know that Dibidale lost her weight cloth and may have been unlucky, but at least she did have a stone less to carry than her rivals in the last furlong. Certainly the ground came right for Dibidale but at the last moment her luck ran out.'

Peter's view is that Dibidale would have had no chance if the rain hadn't eased the going a few hours before the race.

Polygamy then ran in the Irish Sweeps Oaks, but her trainer believed her to be over the top. She was third behind Dibidale.

'She ran a sloppy sort of race,' Peter said. 'She was so small, and we had been very lucky having trained her for the Guineas, to win the Oaks. It was rather like Grundy really. I trained him for the Guineas in which he was beaten, and then he won the Derby. But he had rather more scope than Polygamy. With a little filly like her if you get beaten a short head in one Classic the gods are being very kind to you when you pull out of it after a hard race and go and win your next Classic.'

We next turned to handicaps. I asked Peter if he was keenly interested in them, and if he worried about success or lack of it in them? His answer was, 'I do worry because my horses are nearly always badly handicapped. The trouble is that they are always doing their best. They run up to their mark every time and as they get their full share of weight they are a bit too high in the handicap. Handicaps are so hard to win. In my opinion the horses that win handicaps are those that run inconsistently. These are the horses that win a couple of races a year, then they have a bit of time off, and then a race or two to get them ready in the spring.

'I haven't won many big handicaps. The Victoria Cup has come my way a couple of times, with Town Crier and Record Token, but I am not really geared to win this sort of race. Anyhow I think

A dramatic finish to the 1974 Oaks. Polygamy, left, is the winner from Furioso (near the rails). Willie Carson on Dibidale (between them) is riding a bareback finish. (Sport & General)

(inset) Dibidale's saddle has twisted right round and a stirrup iron can be seen dangling.

from the prestige point of view one goes for the maiden races with the worst horses or you go with the good animals for the condition races, which is where the money lies. We have won nearly a hundred Group races already.' The record bears out Peter's contention. From 1961 to 1977 he had trained winners on the flat under Jockey Club Rules, which had amassed £1,701,879 in first place money.

Peter has spent a considerable proportion of his share of the winnings on improving his property. He has two wood-shaving gallops. Many people call them 'all weather', but not Peter. He believes that when the ground is soft then work on the turf is preferable to that on sodden shavings. 'We've now got these bore holes on the Downs and they are lowering the water table,' he explained. 'This means that the gallops tend to dry up more quickly than before because the water is taken away from below. So that is why we do have the shavings gallops. I have one over a mile and a quarter and the other over six furlongs. They are pretty good. You can keep horses ticking over with the help of these gallops. You can also do fast work on the bridle on them. I can use them in most weathers, but I don't like using them when they are really wet and soft because horses' feet go straight through the shavings.'

Peter is trying hard to improve the turf at Seven Barrows. He has a better chance to do this than in previous years because Barry Hills, who also trains at Lambourn, used to work his horses on Peter's gallops two days a week, but now Barry has a gallop of his own. Thus the number of horses on Peter's gallops has been much reduced and he has a chance to improve them.

'I've got two gallop men, and a mole catcher. I help all three. When we came to Seven Barrows we caught four hundred moles the first year. That was me, really, and the gallop men working flat out with gloves and traps.' Peter's war on moles may seem unkind to some readers but the furry little creatures can play havoc with the gallops. The mole hills plus the weakening of the turf resulting from their tunnels can cause accidents which have been known to be fatal to horses and humans.

Peter has a covered ride which is a great help in training. Whatever the weather he can exercise horses in it for a good hour and a half. It has done a marvellous job for him. It must help him to start the season well, but Lambourn horses as a rule are not very early. With a few individual exceptions they never come to themselves at Seven Barrows until May. There the wind comes nipping in for about five miles straight from the north east and White Horse Hill. In Upper Lambourn they have a big ridge behind them which shields them from the wind.

'It really is a cold old place here,' said Peter. 'We tend to put more buildings up and grow more trees to shelter it, but you cannot keep out the wind the whole time.'

Peter's contention is that if you force horses too much in the spring they won't last the season. Incidentally, they had a super season in 1977 with a hundred and eleven winners—which put the stable third on the list—but its best year was in 1975 when it had a hundred and twenty-five winners. 'We usually celebrate with a party just before Christmas for the lads and stable workers. They are a great team and I am very proud of them,' added Peter.

In view of the fact that more than one trainer I have spoken to in recent years has favoured the American method of employing labour, whereby you have a number of grooms and just a handful of really expert work riders who take over the horses for fast work on the gallops, I asked Peter what he thought of it. He replied, 'I am against it. With a hundred horses you could have eight to a dozen Lots out all through the morning. The chaps would never get a break, but by having two or possibly three Lots out, as we do, you can have your First Lot come in and then the lads are away to their breakfast. They come back for the Second Lot. I can see most of my horses at exercise. Having say ten or a dozen Lots out I simply wouldn't see half of them at work. In theory it is all very well. In America they are guided by the fact that the tracks are closed by ten o'clock in the morning because they have to prepare them for the afternoon's racing.

'I think half the fun for lads in racing is that they don't have to spend most of their time mucking out! If they want to do that they can work on a stud. If they want to be in a racing stable they put up with the mucking out because they love riding out. Also in an entirely understandable and reasonable way they take a strong proprietary interest in the horses they look after.

'A good lad looks after a horse and gets it going sweetly for you. He takes great pride in this. It gets harder to find this type of lad today, but I think that whatever industry you are in it is more difficult to find the keen youngsters who take a pride in their work. The standard seems to be going down the whole time. I am very sad to have to say this because I like the youngsters of today and realise there are some good ones among them.

'I have been told that before World War II, if you sacked a lad in Lambourn you would have five or more round the door the same afternoon wanting the job. They were unemployed and desperate. They were paid two pounds a week. They could live on that because the costs were very low, but they were keen and knew their job. Of course we don't want those unhappy years of the early Thirties back again.

'I think one wants to build up a standard of lads and keep it as high as one can. Mine are controlled and disciplined. They have got to be. You cannot have a place where the boys come in at their own time. Every morning they have to pull out with their horses at 7.30 a.m. into the covered ride. There I can see them all and tell them where they have got to go.

'I think the wage should be higher than it is compared to industry, particularly when you look at the layabouts in some of the factories who seem to be doing absolutely nothing and to be on strike half the time. The more money you give some of these chaps—I don't mean all of them—the less they respect it and they blow it.

'Among my lads the single ones are all right. It's the married ones that worry me. To keep a home going on £50 a week even if they live in a free cottage which a lot of mine do, is not easy. I suppose my lads get about £50–£60 a week.'

Our next subject was racing horses abroad. I asked Peter if he worried about sending them overseas. 'Oh no, not at all,' he replied. 'The planes and motorways make it all so easy. We are very well fixed in this area for communications. The great majority of horses seem to travel very well in a plane. They relax and it's fine. I send horses all over the place but unlike John Dunlop, for example, I have not yet supported Cagnes-sur-Mer, which as you know is near Nice and is held in the late winter and early spring. Most of the trainers who have gone down there have done very well. There is just a chance that horses may pick up some bug which leaves them out of form when they get back to England for the opening of our season. I know that happened to one trainer who for a few weeks had a very worrying time but I'm glad to say that they recovered and his stable had a very good year.

'I have won races at Frankfurt, St Cloud, Deauville, extinct Le Tremblay, lots at Longchamp, and I have had runners at Baden-

It's a chilly March morning as Peter Walwyn's string heads for the gallops at Seven Barrows, Lambourn. (Daily Mirror/Syndication International)

Baden but the going can be very heavy there, as well as winners in Ireland at The Curragh, Leopardstown, and even Tralee.'

'What about apprentices?,' I asked. 'We don't seem to have many,' Peter replied, 'but I have a promising boy at the moment— Nick Howe. I would say that he has a good chance of making a top jockey. He looks like having a future. He comes from Moreton-in-the-Marsh where my sister lives.'

As soon as Pat Eddery was well on the way to becoming champion jockey in 1977 Peter put Nick up on quite a few horses which Pat would have ridden if he had not been virtually champion. Pat did not mind. All being well Nick, who is seventeen, will eventually get plenty of rides.

Peter then went on to pay his jockey Pat Eddery a tribute: 'He has been a marvellous jockey, underrated in my view, because he is in Lester Piggott's shadow. They get on very well and I believe Lester respects Pat more than any other jockey. Lester is always frightened of Pat in a race because Pat has that little bit of genius. In 1977 he had a better average of successful rides than Lester. This was commendable because Lester tends to pick only what he wants to ride. Pat has to ride everything of mine that he can because the owners are paying the retainer. He does as he is told and is no prima donna. He loves riding horses and has a great sympathy with them. He has beautiful hands and is a superb jockey.'

The first winner ridden by Pat for Peter Walwyn was Mrs Eleanor Glazebrook's Silly Symphony at Wolverhampton in 1971. The same owner, who lives in Cheshire and seldom has more than one horse in training with Peter, was also responsible for another milestone in the stable's history—Peter's 1,000th winner, when Huahinee won at Folkestone in March 1978.

The 1978 season began well for Peter. The winning tally soon mounted and he seemed destined to pass the hundred mark, 'as usual' one might say. But the virus struck his string of over one hundred and twenty horses during the summer, and he had to suspend operations for several weeks. He began to win races in the autumn, but by then the season was virtually over.

In April he won the City and Suburban with Saros and the White Rose Stakes with Leonardo da Vinci. In May he took the Jockey Club Stakes with Classic Example, the Lingfield Oaks Trial with Suni, the Ormonde Stakes with Crow and the Prix du Cadran with Buckskin, one of the Daniel Wildenstein horses at Seven Barrows which were switched to Henry Cecil's team after Royal Ascot, where Peter won the Jersey Stakes with Camden Town and the Britannia Stakes with Rhineland. Crow won the Coronation Cup in May.

That, however, was Peter's lot for 1978, as far as big winners was concerned. It will not be long before he is 'on top' once again.

STATISTICAL RECORDS

Peter Walwyn has had 18 complete seasons as a trainer (1961–78) and all figures are for this period. All are Flat unless otherwise stated. He has had 1,030 winners on the Flat under Jockey Club rules, plus 19 winners under N.H. rules, the total for the Flat being £1,890,647 and for jumping £5,416. Including wins abroad his total is well in excess of £2,000,000.

TRAINERS' TABLE

1969	4th	66 winners of	£86,391
1970	3rd	54 winners of	£103,158
1971	7th	61 winners of	£62,660
1972	8th	55 winners of	£60,140
1973	2nd	87 winners of	£123,892
1974	1st	96 winners of	£206,783
1975	1st	121 winners of	£382,527
1976	2nd	110 winners of	£260,112
1977	3rd	110 winners of	£316,564
1978	9th	70 winners of	£188,769

BIG RACES

He won 282 races worth more than £1,000 to the winner up to 1977. In 1978 he won 28 races worth more than £2,000.

U.K. races worth £4,000 or more to the winner (and also including Royal Ascot wins below that amount) were:

1965

YORKSHIRE OAKS	York	Mabel	£4,465

1969

QUEEN ANNE STAKES	Royal Ascot	Town Crier	2,235
CORONATION STAKES	Royal Ascot	Lucyrowe	4,539
YORKSHIRE OAKS	York	Frontier Goddess	5,825
CHEVELEY PARK	Newmarket	Humble Duty	10,187
SUN CHARIOT	Newmarket	Lucyrowe	4,502

1970

ONE THOUSAND GUINEAS	Newmarket	Humble Duty	21,015
CORONATION STAKES	Royal Ascot	Humble Duty	4,577
SUSSEX STAKES	Goodwood	Humble Duty	12,087
GORDON STAKES	Goodwood	Rock Roi	4,143
WILLS MILE	Goodwood	Humble Duty	7,343
OBSERVER GOLD CUP	Doncaster	Linden Tree	19,698

1971			
HARDWICKE STAKES	Royal Ascot	Ortis	£9,662
1972			
JOHN PORTER	Newbury	Rock Roi	4,189
DEWHURST	Newmarket	Lunchtime	13,340
1973			
BESSBOROUGH	Royal Ascot	Loyal Guard	3,252
NORFOLK STAKES	Royal Ascot	Habat	5,199
BRITANNIA	Royal Ascot	Tudor Rhythm	3,946
MILL REEF STAKES	Newbury	Habat	10,026
GREEN SHIELD	Sandown	Cesarea	4,807
MIDDLE PARK	Newmarket	Habat	25,346
PTS LAURELS	Goodwood	Spring Stone	6,636
1974			
TOTE FREE HANDICAP	Newmarket	Charlie Bubbles	4,040
DAILY MIRROR HANDICAP	Epsom	Spring Stone	4,157
OAKS	Epsom	Polygamy	40,079
QUEEN'S VASE	Royal Ascot	Royal Aura	4,402
KING EDWARD VII	Royal Ascot	English Prince	10,727
CHESHAM	Royal Ascot	Red Cross	3,243
CHAMPAGNE	Doncaster	Grundy	9,443
MILL REEF STAKES	Newbury	Red Cross	10,884
WM HILL DEWHURST	Newmarket	Grundy	26,271
HORRIS HILL	Newbury	Corby (USA)	6,855
1975			
LADBROKE DERBY TRIAL	Lingfield	Patch	7,413
THE DERBY	Epsom	Grundy	106,465
HARDWICKE STAKES	Royal Ascot	Charlie Bubbles	12,345
LANCASHIRE OAKS	Haydock	One Over Par	5,098
KING GEORGE VI AND QUEEN ELIZABETH	Ascot	Grundy	81,810
GEOFFREY FREER	Newbury	Consol	8,098
YORKSHIRE OAKS	York	May Hill	13,192
GREAT VOLTIGEUR	York	Patch	9,119
PARKHILL	Doncaster	May Hill	9,085
HORRIS HILL	Newbury	State Occasion	6,618
1976			
LADBROKE BLUE RIBAND TRIAL	Epsom	Oats	4,388
JOCKEY CLUB STAKES	Newmarket	Orange Bay	4,991
HARDWICKE STAKES	Royal Ascot	Orange Bay	14,412
WATERFORD CRYSTAL MILE	Goodwood	Free State	10,720
CAVENDISH CAPE	Ascot	Record Token	8,560
CHAMPION STAKES	Newmarket	Vitiges	38,609
WM HILL FUTURITY	Doncaster	Sporting Yankee	36,398
VERNONS SPRINT	Haydock	Record Token	13,611

1977

WARREN STAKES	Epsom	Millionaire	£4,552
JOCKEY CLUB STAKES	Newmarket	Oats	8,457
ORMONDE STAKES	Chester	Oats	7,271
QUEEN'S VASE	Royal Ascot	Millionaire	6,321
LANCASHIRE OAKS	Haydock	Busaca	11,811
EDWARD VII STAKES	Royal Ascot	Classic Example	14,215
MILL REEF STAKES	Newbury	Formidable (USA)	19,094
CUMBERLAND LODGE	Ascot	Orange Bay	7,310
MIDDLE PARK	Newmarket	Formidable (USA)	19,094
CROWN+TWO FINAL	York	Wind	4,019
WM HILL FUTURITY	Doncaster	Dactylographer (USA)	42,776

1978

NELL GWYN STAKES	Newmarket	Seraphima	6,249
CITY AND SUBURBAN	Epsom	Saros	4,428
AYMERS COFFEE	Ascot	Pamina	4,071
WHITE ROSE	Ascot	Leonardo da Vinci	5,833
JOCKEY CLUB STAKES	Newmarket	Classic Example	10,442
ORMONDE STAKES	Chester	Crow	9,912
OAKS TRIAL	Lingfield	Suni	8,607
CORONATION CUP	Epsom	Crow	25,206
JERSEY	Royal Ascot	Camden Town	7,436
BRITANNIA	Royal Ascot	Rhineland	4,808
IRISH SWEEPS AUTUMN HANDICAP	Newmarket	Proven	8,973

Overseas wins include Irish Sweeps Derby with English Prince and Grundy, Irish Two Thousand Guineas with Grundy.

Repeated wins include:

DON ZOILO STAKES, Sandown	1975, 1976
HARDWICKE STAKES, Royal Ascot	1971, 1975, 1976
JOCKEY CLUB STAKES, Newmarket	1975, 1976, 1977
HORRIS HILL, Newbury	1974, 1975
LOWTHER, York	1969, 1975
YORKSHIRE OAKS, York	1965, 1969, 1975
NEWBURY SPRING CUP, Newbury	1971, 1975
CRAVEN STAKES, Newmarket	1974, 1975
DEWHURST, Newmarket	1972, 1974
DUKE OF EDINBURGH, Ascot	1968, 1974
MILL REEF STAKES, Newbury	1973, 1974, 1977

BEST RACECOURSES

Top courses are spread between South and Midlands. Little in North.

Ascot	67 wins	(excluding Rock Roi, twice 1st and disqualified Ascot Gold Cup)
Newmarket	64 ,,	
Newbury	63 ,,	
Wolverhampton	58 ,,	
Salisbury	54 ,,	
Bath	50 ,,	
Lingfield	46 ,,	
Kempton	44 ,,	
Goodwood	43 ,,	
Sandown	43 ,,	

JOCKEYS

Pat Eddery	512 wins
Duncan Keith	172 ,,
Joe Mercer	80 ,,
Frank Morby	63 ,,
Frank Durr	31 ,,
Nick Howe	10 ,,

More than 60 jockeys have won for him.

BEST MONTHS

August	202 wins
July	162 ,,
June	159 ,,
May	153 ,,

MULTIPLE WINS

To the end of 1977 he has had 139 doubles and 34 trebles. He has had 11 doubles at Wolverhampton. Six doubles, one treble, one mixed treble and four mixed doubles at Chepstow. At Salisbury: six doubles, one treble, one mixed treble and two mixed doubles. Bath: three straight trebles, four mixed trebles, two straight and seven mixed doubles.

OWNERS

Because of husband and wife ownership and partnerships it is difficult to give absolutely clear figures, but Walwyn has had approximately 140 different owners. Leading winners:

Eight Flat-Racing Stables

Louis Freedman	64 (plus Mrs L. Freedman, 1)
Mrs D. McCalmont	64
G. P. Williams	61
E. de Rothschild	58
Dr C. Vittadini	39
A. D. G. Oldrey	33

HORSES

An enormous turnover of winning horses, in the region of 450 of which each of approximately 40 per cent won one race for him. Virtually the only horse to go on winning year after year was the inimitable Be Hopeful, who raced successfully from 1962 to 1973, winning 27 races.

Index

The names of horses are printed in italics.
Page numbers in italics refer to illustrations.

Index

Index

Index